W9-AFK-411

WITHDRAWN
NDSU

Research Studies in Library Science, No. 5

RESEARCH STUDIES IN LIBRARY SCIENCE
Bohdan S. Wynar, Editor

No. 1. *Middle Class Attitudes and Public Library Use.* By Charles Evans; with an Introduction by Lawrence Allen.

No. 2. *Critical Guide to Catholic Reference Books.* By James Patrick McCabe, with an Introduction by Russell E. Bidlack.

No. 3. *An Analysis of Vocabulary Control in Library of Congress Classification and Subject Headings.* By John Phillip Immroth, with an Introduction by Jay E. Daily.

No. 4. *Research Methods in Library Science. A Bibliographic Guide.* By Bohdan S. Wynar.

No. 5. *Library Management: Behavior-Based Personnel Systems. A Framework for Analysis.* By Robert E. Kemper.

Library Management

Behavior - Based

Personnel Systems (BBPS):

A Framework for Analysis

ROBERT E. KEMPER

1971

Libraries Unlimited, Inc., Littleton, Colo.

251713

Copyright © 1971 Robert E. Kemper
All Rights Reserved
Printed in the United States of America

Library of Congress Card Number 73-165063
Standard Book Number 87287-036-7

LIBRARIES UNLIMITED, INC.
P.O. Box 263
Littleton, Colorado 80120

Z
674
RH
nos

PREFACE

Knowledge about administration, organization, and management is not readily transformed by library administrators into improved library personnel practice. Consequently, a vehicle is needed for synthesizing and incorporating new knowledge into brief instructional packages. This book proposes a framework for the broad subject—personnel administration. It is hoped that this framework will be useful to librarians who do research on personnel systems, to those who design them, to those who use them, and to students. As new ideas come to their attention, they need some way of organizing them, of relating them to—or contrasting them with—ideas they have already accepted; and, if they accept the new ideas, of knowing the limits of their applicability. The framework may have collateral benefits to librarians in thinking about job descriptions and organization structure, to library educators in planning courses, and to potential students of administration in developing a personal reading program.

The purpose of the book, then, is not to present how-to-do-it personnel administration techniques. Rather, it proposes to provide a perspective on personnel systems in human organizations; that is, libraries where people are brought together for a common purpose. Three foci provide direction for this book: (1) the nature of personnel administration, (2) the process of skill-level development, and (3) conflict and resolution in library organizations. A major portion of the book is devoted to the environment of personnel problem-solving by use of a detailed case study in human conflict.

It follows that the work is not a substitute for general personnel or management textbooks, library management case books, or other similar materials. Instead, it is only a commentary on such works. It does not profess to comment or recommend through supplemental references on more than a few of what seem to be the most basic. The people for whom the book is intended are most likely librarians first, administrators and supervisors second—by default, circumstance, or advancement.

The conceptualization of BBPS, Behavioral-Based Personnel Systems, is achieved in six chapters. In Chapter I personnel management is placed in perspective relative to the total administrative function. Chapter II presents the concept of an organization as a social system, various approaches to library personnel leadership, the philosophy behind BBPS, and the challenge to library managers. Chapter III is an effort to spell out the terminology and system of concepts for describing variables influencing the behavior of people at work. This particular conceptual scheme provides a tool for analyzing the cause-and-effect relationship that results in organizational conflict. Basic skill requirements underlying administrative functions are covered in Chapter IV. The case study presented in Chapter V provides an analysis "walk-through" which may be useful in personnel problem-solving.

The case is divided into various parts to provide an opportunity for heuristic problem-solving. Each phase of the case is followed by study guide questions relating to administrative and human relations skill development. It is suggested that the case be analyzed section by section according to the selected breakdown. The final chapter, Chapter VI, develops the functional relationship between behavioral based personnel planning and strategic long-range library planning, discusses the tools of personnel problem-solving and summarizes the conceptualization of BBPS.

TABLE OF CONTENTS

PREFACE 5

CHAPTER I.   NATURE OF PERSONNEL
              ADMINISTRATION 11
THE CONCEPTUALIZATION OF PERSONNEL ADMINISTRATION. 12
A NEED FOR A PROPER PERSPECTIVE ON THE PERSONNEL
    PROCESS 12
FOOTNOTES 13
BASIC REFERENCES 14

CHAPTER II. PEOPLE, BEHAVIOR, SYSTEMS 15
VARIOUS APPROACHES TO LIBRARY PERSONNEL
    LEADERSHIP 16
      The Kindly Library Administrator 16
      The Disinterested Library Leader 16
      The "All Is Well That Ends Well" Approach . 16
THE BBPS POSITION 17
THE CHALLENGE TO LIBRARY MANAGERS 17
FOOTNOTES 18
BASIC REFERENCES 18

CHAPTER III.   CONCEPTUALIZATION OF BEHAVIOR-
               BASED PERSONNEL SYSTEMS 19
BEHAVIOR-BASED MODEL OF ORGANIZATION CONFLICT 19
ELEMENTS OF WORK BEHAVIOR 19
ENVIRONMENTAL CONSTRAINTS DETERMINING REQUIRED
    AND GIVEN BEHAVIOR 22
      External Environmental Factors 22
      Institutional and Library Environmental Factors 22
      Technological Environmental Factors 22
      Personal Background Factors 22
EMERGENT BEHAVIOR 23
ORGANIZATIONAL IMAGE 23
CONFLICT RESULUTION 24
FOOTNOTES 24
BASIC REFERENCES 25

CHAPTER IV.   A FRAMEWORK FOR SKILL-LEVEL
              DEVELOPMENT 26
ESSENTIAL SKILLS 28
THE SUPERVISORY SKILL-MIX 29

FOOTNOTES 32
BASIC REFERENCES 32

CHAPTER V.   BEHAVIORAL ENVIRONMENT:
                        PRAIRIE STATE COLLEGE LIBRARY . . 33
PRAIRIE STATE COLLEGE LIBRARY 34
PERSONAL BACKGROUNDS 39
THOUGHT QUESTIONS (PART 1) 44
A NEW STAFF MEMBER 45
REQUIRED BEHAVIOR 47
THOUGHT QUESTIONS (PART 2) 54
PERSONAL CONFLICT 55
EMERGENT BEHAVIOR 57
THOUGHT QUESTIONS (PART 3) 59
A CONFLICT OF VALUES 60
FINANCIAL CRISIS 66
REQUIRED BEHAVIOR 69
THOUGHT QUESTIONS (PART 4) 70
EXCERPTS 71
    Annual Report of the Acquisitions Librarian of Eberhard
       Library on the Operations and Conditions of the
       Acquisitions Department 71
    Acquisitions Organization, Policies, and Procedures Manual,
       Eberhard Library, Prairie State College 74
THOUGHT QUESTIONS (SUMMARY) 78
FOOTNOTES 79
BASIC REFERENCES 79

CHAPTER VI.   EFFECTIVE PERSONNEL MANAGE-
                        MENT: TODAY AND TOMORROW 80
THE FUNCTION OF MANAGERIAL INFORMATION 80
INFORMATION GATHERING 82
SUMMARY 83
FOOTNOTES 85
READINGS FOR FUTURE EXPLORATION 86

APPENDIX A.   NOTES ON PERSONNEL PROCESSES . . 88
THE PERSONNEL MANAGEMENT PROCESSES 88
    The Leadership Process 88
    The Justice-Determination Process 88
    The Task-Specialization Process 89
    The Staffing Process 89
    The Appraisal Process 89
    The Compensation Process 90
    The Collective-Bargaining Process 90
    The Organizational Training and Development Process 90

**APPENDIX B.   CURRENT LIBRARY MANPOWER
PHILOSOPHY AND B.B.P.S.** 91
THE TASK APPROACH 91
TASKS PERFORMED *ONLY* BY PERSONNEL IN PARTICULAR
PAID STAFF POSITIONS 91
    Elementary-School Library Media Centers 92
    Secondary-School Library Media Centers 94
THE NORMATIVE APPROACH 94
LIBRARY EDUCATION AND MANPOWER
    A Statement of Policy Adopted by the Council of the
    American Library Association, June 30, 1970 94
THE COLOR BOOK APPROACH 103
FOOTNOTES 104

CHAPTER I

NATURE OF PERSONNEL ADMINISTRATION

Selection and acquisition, cataloging and classification, reference service, and circulation of materials are the traditional library functions. Librarians also are administrators and supervisors, and a few of them direct large library organizations with annual operating expenditures of a million dollars or more. Current demands on librarianship have been shown to be immensely challenging. There are certainly many librarians[1] and library specialists who are indeed presented with the opportunity, both in their day-to-day work and in their other professional activities, to deal with the urgent problems which face the library profession. It is also clear that not all library positions offer these opportunities.[2] The lack of challenging work, faulty formal organizations, unsatisfactory personnel policies or procedures, existence of function relationships that are unsound or misunderstood, poor communication, and unfair supervisory practices cause library personnel to think about leaving the profession as well as a particular library. When possible, the conditions that foster job and profession dissatisfaction should be corrected.

Human resources in the library are used more effectively and efficiently in the accomplishment of the library organization's goals now than in the pre-ALA standards or the pre-academic rank and status era. By no means have the problems been solved. The solution to library oriented personnel problems can be minimized by:

1. Developing job functions that are properly assigned to clerical man-power who are paid at a lower rate than costly professionals.
2. Studying task definitions and classifications to facilitate full use of professional staff and to restructure the total staff to fit available manpower.
3. Identifying skills necessary to perform tasks at different levels of responsibility.
4. Attending to personality, educational and experience factors needed to perform library functions.
5. Developing effective training programs for the upgrading of presently employed library manpower.
6. Developing education programs that focus upon administrative, human relations, and technical skills of a supervisor.
7. Planning accelerated recruitment programs for new manpower.
8. Recruiting personnel with appropriate technical, human relations, and administrative skills.

9. Bringing about the congruency between library goals and employee freedom to exercise initiative.

10. Developing policies and procedures that will enable library supervisors to motivate clerical members toward desired goals and at the same time maintain an appropriate level of discipline and job performance.

11. Bringing about effective communication between the librarian and the administration and between the many faculty members and specialists.

12. Preparing library students for administrative and supervisor positions.

The art and science of rational personnel decision-making permits a way to frame and analyze such complex personnel problems. Current administrative thought forms a basis for a systems-based approach to library personnel planning.

THE CONCEPTUALIZATION OF PERSONNEL ADMINISTRATION

The personnel process[3] involves the recruitment, selection, utilization, and development of human resources by and within the organization. Human resources in the library consist of personnel available as members of the library organization—administration, faculty, facilitating staff, and students. Personnel administration can be effective to the degree that it contributes to the goals of the library. The main objective of the library administrator is to give the highest quality service within the limitations of available financial resources. It is through the personnel process that a sufficient and trained professsional and subject specialist staff is assembled to organize and administer the resources of the library.

Personnel administration is a major component of the broad administrative function. It is concerned with human behavior, sentiments, interactions, activities, and values. As such, it is more than just the management of people by library supervisors, academic library department heads, public library administrators, personnel officers, or government officials.

A NEED FOR A PROPER PERSPECTIVE ON THE PERSONNEL PROCESS

Efforts to describe and analyze the librarian's job suffer from the same difficulties encountered in dealing with the role of the public administrator. There is a desire to treat library positions like other professional positions involving lengthy study, technical knowledge, and a code of ethics. The practicing librarian, graduate library school faculty member, the state library consultant, and so forth, for the sake of prestige, identification, and self-justification, want to consider librarianship a profession—an appropriate objective.

Professionalism, however, is but one facet of a job. The public administrator must understand the day-to-day nature and functions of his organization: public policy, budgeting, staffing, fiscal and other operating controls. Just as the public administrator must be informed on basic organizational operations, so must the library administrator be cognizant of the nature and functions of the library organization—material sources, library patrons, curriculum design, learning processes. Most important for the library administrator and the public administrator, however, is the ability to deal with people.

The necessity of dealing with people focuses on human relations skill. There is a tendency to treat this operational skill[4] separately, that is, distinguished from the professional aspects of the job. Skill, after all, implies intuition, sensitivity, and a feeling for the situation. Human relations skill has been treated as an inborn trait or an art—one not requiring extensive study at the graduate library program level. It is easier to envision a profession in terms of knowledge and service than of human behavior. The exclusion of the human element presents an unrealistic view of the librarian's job, a view that will not foster easy attainment of library goals.

The library administrator must assure that resources are obtained and used effectively in the accomplishment of the institution's[5] goals. This operational process conveys three key ideas. First, supervisors must get things accomplished by working with other people. Second, the process takes place within the context of goals and policies established by the higher organizational administration. Third, effectiveness and efficiency determine the action to take.

Library educators may downgrade or ignore the human relations aspects of the librarian's job, perhaps because they interfere with the professionalsim of librarianship. Human resource aspects challenge the librarian's professional status in two ways. First, the dealing with people aspect of the supervisor's job appears to represent functions not as clear-cut and definable as the librarian's technical activities; and second, there is a noteworthy failure to define the. task aspect of the librarian's job.

In Chapter II the concept of systems is related to social (people) organizations and the process of personnel decision-making. Emphasis will be on perspective, not on universally applicable solutions or final answers.

FOOTNOTES

[1] In this book, the librarian will be called a librarian, not a media specialist or media director, a resource teacher, an instructional media supervisor, or any other labels popular among educators used to convey an expanded concept of the library's function.

[2] Anita R. Schiller, "What Librarians Do and What They Think," in *Reader in the Academic Library,* edited by Michael M. Reynolds. (Washington: NCR Microcard Editions, 1970), pp. 228-237.

[3] The word "process" is defined as a flow of interrelated events moving toward some goal, purpose, or end. The personnel process is usually conceived as consisting of the task specialization process, the staffing process, the appraisal process, the training and development process, the compensation process, and the leadership process. (See Appendix A for a discussion and definitions.)

[4] Operational skill is defined as the ability to obtain and use resources effectively and efficiently in the accomplishment of the organization's goals. The human relations skill conceives effective and efficient use of human resources.

[5] An institution, as defined in this book, refers to a college, university, school system, municipality, state or federal agency in which the library operates.

BASIC REFERENCES

French, Wendell. *The Personnel Management Process,* 2d. ed. (Boston: Houghton-Mifflin Company, 1970), pp. 3-8.

Kemper, Robert E. "Library Planning: The Challenge of Change" in *Advances in Librarianship,* Vol. 1. Edited by Melvin J. Voigt (New York: Academic Press, 1970), pp. 207-239.

National Education Association, Division of Research. *School Library Personnel Task Analysis: A Report Prepared in Phase I of the School Library Manpower Project by the Research Division of the National Education Association in a National Study to Identify the Tasks Performed by School Library Personnel in Unified Service Programs at the Building Level* (Chicago: American Library Association, 1969).

Sayles, Leonard. *Managerial Behavior* (New York: McGraw-Hill, 1964).

Stone, Elizabeth W. "Administrators Fiddle While Employees Burn or Flee," *ALA Bulletin,* 63:181-187 (February, 1969).

Wasserman, Paul and Mary Lee Bundy. *A Program of Research Into the Indentfication of Manpower Requirements, the Educational Preparation and the Utilization of Manpower in the Library and Infromation Professions.* Final Report, Phase I (College Park: University of Maryland, School of Library and Information Services, January, 1969, Project No. 7-1804).

CHAPTER II

PEOPLE, BEHAVIOR, SYSTEMS

The concept of an organization as a social system has received considerable attention in recent years.[1] The social-system approach looks upon administration as a system of cultural interrelationships. The concept of a social system draws heavily on sociology, anthropology, management, political science, economics, and psychology. It involves recognition of such elements as formal and informal organization within a totally integrated system. Moreover, the organization or enterprese is recognized as a product of external pressure or conflict from the cultural environment.

As indicated in Chapter I, personnel administration is an approach to effective and efficient use of human resources in an organization. A systems-based approach to personnel administration and the planning that results from it is not an end in itself, but rather, is a means to an end. The desired end, of course, is improved library service. As a means to that end a systems-based approach provides library decision makers with a framework for systematically relating organizational activities to organizational activities to organizational goals and objectives.

As generally used, systems refers to "a particular linking of components which has a facilitating effect, or an intended facilitating effect, on the carrying out of a process."[2] The systems approach to personnel administration is concerned with the question of how to achieve a given end and how it results in decisions about human activities and behavior.

In a systems approach context, however, personnel administration takes on a more specific definition because a decision-maker must be concerned with developing not only such components as materials, techniques, procedures, plans, policies and rules, but also people.

Thus, the library organization reflects the motives and aspirations of library personnel as modified extensively by socio-cultural factors. Since man is a social creature, he takes most of his sentiments and norms of conduct from other members of society. Certainly a society which places high value upon human decency, and is geared primarily to the satisfaction of basic needs, must give adequate recognition to the impact of people upon library organizations.

Traditional library personnel administration has involved the identificatin of professional library education programs in graduate library schools and the recruitement, selection, and utilization of these graduates by libraries. A graduate qualifies as a librarian because he has an M.L.S. (Master of Library Science). He has completed a prescribed core of course work and thus is qualified for a professional library career.

As suggested, however, there is an alternative approach to personnel administration. It takes into account not only the required activities sentiments, and interactions of librarians within an organization, but also the cause-and-effect relationship between these behavioral requirements and emergent behavior. The use of "intended facilitating effect" in the above systems' definition purposely suggests that mistakes may be made in the design of a system so that personal goals are substituted for library goals. Libraries, thus, could become collections of librarians rather than collections of materials.

Essentially, then, there must be an attempt to distinguish between personnel administration which takes its cues from traditional graduate library education and placement on the one hand and personnel administration which takes its cues from behavioral aspects on the other. The Behavior Based Personnel Systems (BBPS) approach, a title for the concept suggested in this book, is a behavioral oriented approach to library organization, a "people" approach.

VARIOUS APPROACHES TO LIBRARY PERSONNEL LEADERSHIP

Much has been written about behavioral approaches to personnel administration and its adaptability to library organizations. The most important aspect of BBPS is neither its logic, structure, not its definition; but rather, the spirit and the philosophy which motivate it. When used as a basis for personnel decision-making BBPS eliminates the following administrative images.

THE KINDLY LIBRARY ADMINISTRATOR

This library leader is interested in library personnel in a kindly sort of way. His concern for library personnel is reflected in the things he does for library personnel to satisfy his own ego. He may push for faculty rank and status. He may go for dynamic programs that attract attention. His philosophy finds expression in doing things he *thinks* that his employees want.

THE DISINTERESTED LIBRARY LEADER

This administrator is not interested in people except as a means for rising in the profession and elevating his status. He is a consultant and a subject expert. He travels widely and frequents association conferences. His motivating philosophy is expressed in the phrase "shape up or ship out." The guiding policy on communication is found in a professional "code of ethics."

THE "ALL IS WELL THAT ENDS WELL" APPROACH

This person has no conscious philosophy of human relations. He is neither disinterested nor kindly. He realizes that people must be around to get things done. As long as circulation increases, the budget is not cut, and comparative library statistics places his library in a favorable position, he assumes that "in the end personnel problems will take care of themselves." It does not occur to him that for effective service, people require at least as much expert attention as do machinery and equipment.

THE BBPS POSITION

An effective library leader views his reward and satisfaction in terms of helping individuals realize all that is within their capacity to achieve. He recognizes that an employee is a human being entitled to the respect and consideration which one honorable person automatically extends to another. His position is that:

1. People are indispensable in carrying out goals of the library.
2. No two people are the same in terms of physical fitness, skill, talent, character, knowledge, aptitude, interest, capability, and human motivation.
3. People are highly adaptable in response to their environment— whether good or bad.
4. People must be recruited, selected, utilized, and developed as individuals.
5. To be among the silent majority means to be among the dead.
6. No two, or ten, or two hundred make up a minority.
7. Men require majority opinions as men carry clubs—for security.
8. People are people.

If BBPS as a planning tool is to have any value, the ideas presented must be complemented by a compatible philosophy of human decency. These realizations must be complemented by compatible operational personnel policies and procedures. Library administrators must make sure that actual daily work experiences are a confirmation—rather than a contradiction—of human decency. The way people are treated on the job will be reflected in the form of government they choose.

THE CHALLENGE TO LIBRARY MANAGERS

The major personnel adminstration consideration is improvement of library service. Regardless of how inherently pleasing kindly library administration may be, both library objectives and personal goal satisfaction must be congruent. Consequently, the library supervisor would be advised to (1) decide on what services are desired by library patrons, (2) recruit, select, utilize, and develop at all levels those people who have skills and capacities most appropriate to the particular library, and (3) create an organization in which the congruency between personal goal satisfaction and the library goal attainment is enchanced in such a way as to maximize the attainment of the role of libraries in society.

In Chapter III the basic requirements underlying BBPS are considered. The model conceptualizes the library organization by interrelating the concepts of required and emergent organizational behavior.

FOOTNOTES

[1] For example, see the summary and report of the present state of knowledge about human organizations as presented in March, James G. (ed.), *Handbook of Organizations* (Chicago: Rand McNally and Company, 1965).

[2] Wendell, French, *The Personnel Management Process* (Boston: Houghton-Mifflin Company, 1964), p. 46.

BASIC REFERENCES

Etzioni, Amitai. *Modern Organizations* (Englewood, N.J.: Prentice-Hall, 1964).

French, Wendell. *The Personnel Management Process,* 2d. ed. (Boston: Houghton-Mifflin Company, 1970), pp. 33-43, 99-127, 130-148.

Johnson, Richard A., Fremont E. Kast, and James E. Rosenzweig. *The Theory and Management of Systems,* 2d. ed. (New York: McGraw-Hill, 1967), pp. 3-130, 365-399.

CHAPTER III

CONCEPTUALIZATION OF BEHAVIOR-BASED PERSONNEL SYSTEMS

The conception that behavior is determined by external and internal organizational factors lends itself readily to the analysis of conflict situations. Clearly, the constellation of factors which impinge on a situation at any given moment finds many forces acting in opposition to one another. If conflict is defined as the collision of incompatible forces within a particular time sequence, no person is ever free of conflict. A person at any given moment has the possibility of moving in one of many different directions. Thus, any particular action is the result of some implicit resolution of conflict.

To aid in understanding human behavior under various given organizational conditions, a more systematic way of relating the various elements involved in conflict is needed. This also will aid in understanding the functions which each element of an individual or group's behavior performs in relation to the whole. This chapter presents a conceptualization of the variables which are necessary in analyzing and predicting the behavior of members of work groups, as influenced by such factors as the nature of the task, the technology, and administration's policy and practice. Here is a frame of reference which can greatly increase the understanding and skill with which library employees can be administered, jobs designed, and conflict resolved. A case study presented in Chapter V permits the reader to practice the application of BBPS in an effort to make it operational.

BEHAVIOR-BASED MODEL OF ORGANIZATION CONFLICT

The behavioral-based model depicted in Figure 1 represents well-known systems models used in studying group behavior.[1] In terms of organizational conflict, this model is particularly useful for it distinguishes among the major causes of conflict—external environmental factors; institutional environmental factors; technological factors; personal background factors; required and given behavior; emergent behavior; and resultant image.

ELEMENTS OF WORK BEHAVIOR

In order to understand BBPS, one must look at the different elements of human behavior. This permits a study of the way these elements are related to each other. Three major elements have been defined by those working in the field: activities, interactions, and sentiments. These terms are helpful in analyzing the interrelationship between normative (required) behavior and actual (emergent) behavior.

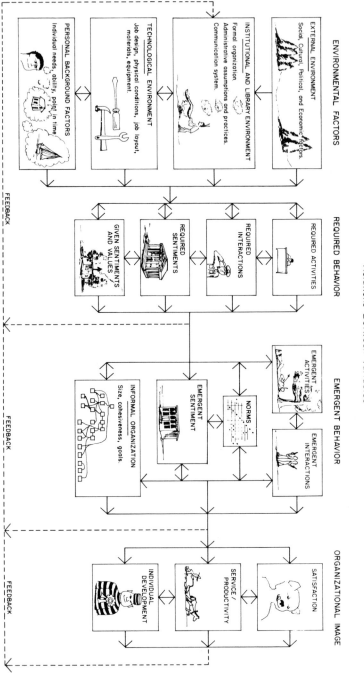

Figure 1

BEHAVIORAL-BASED PERSONNEL SYSTEM
Relations Between Variables

20

Required behavior is administrative oriented behavior, i.e., job descriptions, work rules, personnel policies. Emergent behavior is externally oriented as it depicts behavior beyond the demands of the organization. Where groups are involved in controlling emergent behavior of individuals and small groups, norms develop and may upset the equilibrium between formal and informal organizations. The basic vocabulary of the model includes the following terms:

Activity. An activity is what a library employee does, i.e., he talks, manipulates machinery, catalogs books, answers questions, and so forth.

Interaction. An interaction is a communication or contact between two persons so that the activity of one responds to the activity of the other. Interactions will vary in length as well as importance. In observing interactions it is critical to note by whom they are initiated and the number of people involved.

Sentiment. A sentiment is an idea, belief, or feeling about library tasks and others involved in carrying them out. Sentiments are not easily covered in a matter of pages nor are they directly observable. Sentiments such as, "I cannot stand children," or, "The head librarian is a dogmatic autocrat," can be inferred from observed activity and interaction, or from expressed responses to specific questions, but cannot be observed at first hand.

Required sentiment. A required sentiment is a belief or feeling which a library employee must have in order to perform the task assigned. A children's librarian, for instance, might be required to enjoy children as well as books.

Given sentiment. Given sentiment is a belief or feeling which a library employee brings with him to the organization as a result of his professional and personal background. A professional librarian has a given professional belief as to his role in an organization. This may be in direct conflict with the required sentiments as stipulated by a given library administrator.

Value. When given sentiments pertain to ideals and aspirations which are desirable but impossible to realize absolutely, they are defined as values. Values, thus, are unlimited ideas of what is desirable. The belief that each individual's opinion be taken seriously and be given appropriate weight is vital to the professional librarian. The degree a library director lives up to or represents this value is important in determining the director's status in the eyes of the subordinate.

Norm. A norm is an emergent sentiment—an idea or belief about what the sentiments, activities, or interactions in a particular library group should be. Norms may develop in any subordinate group. They serve to define how intra-group members should behave in relation to outsiders, other group members, the job, and the emergent nonwork activities. For example, civil service workers may limit nonwork interactions with professional librarians on the job. Norms thus control behavior of certain groups in relation to certain other groups.

The definitions, which have purposely been simplified, suggest that behavior which emerges in an organization is different from behavior that is required. This is the starting point from which the important relationships between people in library organizations can be observed. Organizational conflict comes about because of differences in personal backgrounds, required activities, required interactions, required sentiments, technology, physical work conditions, leadership behavior, and so forth. An outline discussion of the various factors follows.

ENVIRONMENTAL CONSTRAINTS DETERMINING REQUIRED AND GIVEN BEHAVIOR

If BBPS, as an operational planning tool, is to have any value in conflict resolution, practical constraints must be buffered against the required activities, interactions, and sentiments which are desirable.

EXTERNAL ENVIRONMENTAL FACTORS

Broad social, cultural, political, and economic factors will affect required behavior primarily through their influence on administrative planning and policy. In particular, the external environmental factors will determine the system of incentives used in the institutional and library organization.

INSTITUTIONAL AND LIBRARY ENVIRONMENTAL FACTORS

Organizational change and conflict are directly affected by three organizational systems: (1) the formal organization, (2) the administrative assumptions and practices, and (3) the communications system.

The elements of the formal organization include the organizational structure, the leadership climate, the organizational efficiency, and personnel policies. Among the personnel elements are the job content, selection procedures, placement procedures, job orientation, work standards, wage and salary level, work incentives, job evaluation, performance rating, and training.

Communications within the organization play an important and vital role by linking the goals of the organization to the goals of the various sources of organizational conflict. The choosing of a leadership pattern from among such alternatives as *laissez-faire,* autocratic, democratic, or a combination of these will have an enormous effect on employee behavior.

TECHNOLOGICAL ENVIRONMENTAL FACTORS

Required behavior also will be affected by technological factors—job design, physical conditions, job layout, and materials. The image of the library is determined to a large extent by facility and resource planning.

PERSONAL BACKGROUND FACTORS

The given sentiments and emergent behavior of organizational members requires a careful analysis of individual needs, ability, and point in time. Physiological, social, and egoistic needs require administrative attention. These will be determined, in large part, by on-job and off-job activities, perception of the situation, level of aspiration, reference groups, cultural background, education and experience.

Individual ability will be determined by aptitude, personality, skills, and knowledge. The general economic conditions of society and the individual's personal situation at a particular point in time will determine how the individual reacts to required behavior.

EMERGENT BEHAVIOR

Organizational behavior viewed only from what is given and required has limited value. The actual behavior of employees is far more complex and meaningful. An understanding of emergent behavior is useful to the extent that it allows the administrator to predict concrete behavior. An administrator must monitor emergent behavior to appriase himself of how his relationship with subordinate groups is proceeding and to identify stresses and strains that may require his intervention.

The administrator's leadership behavior largely involves contacts in which he endeavors to secure a response. This activity is complicated in that an individual employee can belong to several informal groups, can be deviant from any group, or can be isolated from any group.

The administrator must consider the size, the cohesiveness, and goals of informal groups and relate them to background constraints and required behavior. Any propositions which he derives must be consistent with a system of interrelated hypotheses as no part makes much sense without an understanding of the whole.

ORGANIZATIONAL IMAGE

Personnel administration serves the function of relating the goals of the library with the basic and shared values of its personnel. Efforts to maintain the integrity of the library will be governed by what is necessary to project and perpetuate the image of unique wholeness. The congruency between personal goal satisfaction and library goal attainment can cause serious conflicts. The behavioral-based personnel system offers a tool whereby a deliberate effort is made to maximize (1) library service, (2) job satisfaction, and (3) individual development.

Providing library service depends in a large part on the productivity of library personnel. Effective and efficient service results from the social structure of the organization. This structure will preserve the norms emergent from informal activity and interaction. Any administrative change which threatens a group's emergent behavior is likely to influence productivity or service.

Relationships and nonwork activities which emerge in a group will strongly influence the satisfaction which group members derive from their work experience. It is possible, then, to have high productivity and low job satisfaction or high job satisfaction and low productivity. The relationship between productivity and satisfaction depends on the complexities of background elements, required and given behavior.

Individual development is a third consequence of work-group behavior. Library organizations will vary greatly in the extent to which they encourage or limit their members' needs to learn, grow, and develop as individual human beings. In any organization there emerges a pattern of interaction, sentiment, and activity which allows members to fulfill their own potentialities, goals, and rewards. High productivity and job satisfaction does not insure high individual growth. Individual development may be severely limited while satisfaction and productivity are high. Outside activities could bring about such a situation, i.e., being elected to the presidency of the library staff association, being a member of the academic community with full faculty status and rank.

A perceptive interpretation of the observable consequences of work-group behavior will make it possible to structure more intelligently those background factors which library administrators can directly influence.

CONFLICT RESOLUTION

Although the BBPS model has limited value for strategic[2] long-range planning, cause-and-effect analysis based on this model can be applied fruitfully in a library to several kinds of operational planning decisions. For instance, even in its simplest form, it is quite possible to change from a democratic to autocratic leadership pattern to determine the effects on job satisfaction. The feedback loop allows a simple schema for library decision-making by indicating variations in background factors which are related to the organizational image. Over time, library administrators could measure the effects of requiring professional librarians to type sets of catalog cards as a result of the institution's decision to decrease money allocated for clerical typists. As library administrators collect data on the relationship between required activities and actual activities, they are able to use the data to make new judgments about the personnel that will be required to achieve desired library service.

Armed with an adequate theoretical framework into which practical behavioral research can be hung, the administrator is ready to design a personnel information system sufficient to carry out the processes of recruitment, selection, utilization, and development of human resources.

Setting aside for the moment the conceptualization of BBPS, Chapter IV will consider the basic skill requirements underlying administrative functions. Such requirements must incorporate a way of viewing the library orgniazation and decision-making.

FOOTNOTES

[1] See George C. Homans, *The Human Group* (New York: Harcourt, Brace and Company, 1950); H. W. Riecken and G. C. Homans, "Psychological Aspects of Social Structure," in Gardner Lindzey (ed.) *Handbook of Psychology* (Cambridge: Adison-Wesley Publishing Company, 1954), Vol. II, pp. 786-832; Robert A. Sutermeister, *People and Productivity,* 2d. ed. (New York: McGraw-Hill, 1969), pp. 1-65.

[2] Strategic planning is the process of deciding on library goals, changes in these goals, on the resources used to obtain these goals, and on the top administrative policies that are to govern the acquisition, use, and disposition of these resources.

BASIC REFERENCES

Stone, Elizabeth W. *Factors Related to the Professional Development of Librarians* (Metuchen, Scarecrow Press, 1969).

Sutermeister, Robert A. *People and Productivity,* 2d. ed. (New York: McGraw-Hill, 1969), pp. 1-65, 83-103, 104-109, 395-406, 450-459.

CHAPTER IV

A FRAMEWORK FOR SKILL-LEVEL DEVELOPMENT

There is some question in the minds of those who come face to face with librarians or depend upon the services of librarians as to the skill competence that should be required in performance of duties. Even more questionable is the curriculum needed to teach these skills. Library services for changing informational, cultural, educational, and recreational needs require different responsibilities.

The diversity of job responsibilities in library programs, the proliferation of library and media materials, the rapid rate of advancement of library school graduates (as director, associate or assistant librarian, department head, branch head, building librarian, district librarian), and the expanded program of services required by educational innovation are changing the role of librarians. There is a need to recognize the different skill levels and to provide an educational program in line with the library services and the skills required to perform these services.

While all librarians must have some minimum technical, human-relations, and administrative skill, the mix of these skills will vary by organizational level and from library to library. What is the effective skill mix for librarians at one level may not be an effective skill mix for librarians at another level. What is an effective combination at one time may not be an effective combination at a later period.[1]

Traditionally, a librarian's job, no matter what the level, has been task centered.[2] This approach determined the need for know-how competency. Any proposal to design new job descriptions based upon effective combination of tasks and responsibilities and to reorder education and training to prepare individuals for the newly defined jobs cannot be solely task-orientated.[3] This will not solve today's problems. A librarian must assume responsiblity for the administration, supervision, planning, and integration and coordination of a variety of services. Since people are the main ingredient in library organizations and services, library educational training must be people rather than task centered. Personnel administrators in libraries must be behaviorally oriented. This will necessitate thoughtful study of tasks performed by human beings and machines and not human beings as machines.

Within the past two decades the development of computers and planning systems concepts have also occurred and have transformed library activities. To understand the significance of these innovations better Herbert Simon sets forth traditional and modern decision-making methods (see Table 1). This may require the reader to assume that the terms "decision-making" and "management" are somewhat synonymous. Since Herbert Simon advocates (in the author's opinion) that if one knew how managers made decisions we would know all there is to know about management, this assumption is proper.

TABLE 1

TRADITIONAL AND MODERN TECHNIQUES OF DECISION-MAKING

| | Decision-making Techniques | |
	Traditional	Modern

Programmed:
  Routine, repetitive
    decisions
  Organization develops
    specific processes for
    handling them
	1. Habit
	2. Clerical routine: Standard
	    operating procedures
	3. Organization structure:
	    Common expectations
	    A system of sub-goals
	    Well-defined informational
	    channels
		1. Operations research:
		    Mathematical
		      analysis
		    Models
		    Computer
		      simulation
		2. Electronic data
		    processing

Non-programmed:
  One-shot, ill-structured,
    novel policy decisions
  Handled by general
    problem-solving
    processes
	1. Judgment, intuition,
	    creativity
	2. Rules of thumb
	3. Selection and training of
	    executives
		Heuristic problem-
		  solving techniques
		  applied to:
		  (a) Training human
		      decision-makers
		  (b) Constructing
		      heuristic com-
		      puter programs

Source: Herbert A. Simon, *The New Science of Management Decision* (New York: Harper and Row, 1960), p. 8.

Herbert Simon breaks down all administrative decisions and planning into two broad types—programmed and nonprogrammed—and defines them as follows:

> Decisions are programmed to the extent that they are repetitive and routine, to the extent that a definite procedure has been worked out for handling them so they won't have to be treated *de novo* each time they occur . . .
> Decisions are nonprogrammed to the extent that they are novel, unstructured, and consequential. There is no cut-and-dried method for handling the problem because it hasn't arisen before, or because it is so important that it deserves a custom-tailored treatment.[4]

This concept of programmed-nonprogrammed decision-making add a new dimension to skill-level development. Essentially it means that certain activities are programmed—based upon organizational procedures and clerical routines, while others are nonprogrammed—based upon judgment, creativity, and general problem-solving.

Organizational policies and procedures and vocational training provide the major vehicles for dealing with programmed skills. For non-programmed skills the development of judgment is cultivated by professional education, selection, and training. There are obviously many psychological and sociological processes involved in nonprogrammed activities.

ESSENTIAL SKILLS

Library educational programs should receive its cues from a skill-mix framework. It can be shown that a librarian must have administrative competency to perform functions required to coordinate the activities and resources of the library. To integrate institutional objectives with individual employee and user needs, the librarian must have human-relations competency. To accomplish his other assigned tasks, including selection and acquisition, cataloging and classification, reference service, and circulation, the librarian must possess technical competency.

The following definitions, based upon the conceptual framework of those studying and researching the leadership role in formal organizations, give perspective as to the scope of three skills:

Technical skills. Technical skill refers to the ability to use pertinent knowledge, methods, techniques, and equipment necessary for the performance of specific tasks and activities, and for the direction of such performance. Technical skill involves an understanding and proficiency with respect to a specific class of functions in the library organization. These include not only clerical skills (programmed) but also the professional orientations and basic frames of reference (nonprogrammed) that are normally associated with librarian roles and affiliations.[5]

Medical doctors are skillful technicians. Lawyers place emphasis on technical skills. To be sure, each face decisions of both a programmed (routine) and nonprogrammed (judgment) nature. It follows then, that professional librarians should not spend their energies arguing as to whether librarianship is or is not a profession. It only should matter that needed skills are developed. Technical skills can be acquired through formal training in professional schools, informal on-the-job training, or combinations of academic and internship or apprenticeship programs. In recent years, however, informal on-the-job training as a source for nonprogrammed technical skill training has been limited by legislation, standards, and norms which specify the need for completion of planned formal programs of education.

Human relations skill. Human relations skill refers to the ability to use pertinent knowledge and methods for working with people and through people. An understanding of the general principles of human behavior, particularly those principles which involve the regulation of interpersonal relations and human motivation, is needed. The skillful utilization of this understanding in day-to-day interaction with others is imperative.

The librarian with human relations skills understands how the principles of behavior affect not only others but himself as well. In order to get things done through others, the library administrator is sensitive to the frames of reference of himself and others. He realizes that one's attitudes, beliefs, opinions, needs, aspirations, and values color perceived and assumed reality. Vital to the human relations skill is the ability to integrate the goals of library employees and patrons with the goals and objectives of the library. It is essential that the administrator be able to represent the needs and goals of librarians at different levels in the organization to each other so that each can comprehend the problems faced by the other.[6]

It is not uncommon for a graduate librarian to have difficulty in adjusting to the realities of library situations. This difficulty may well stem from the fact that his library courses dealt primarily with tehcnical competence, and he therefore was unaware of—or inadequately aware of—the existence of the operational process and of the distinction between this process and technical processes.

Administrative skill. Administrative skill refers to the ability of the librarian to think and act in terms of the total system within which he operates—in terms of the organization as a system of people and physical objects, with its own image, structure, and process which functions as a continuing complex problem-solving arrangement to attain particular objectives. The emphasis here is on understanding and acting according to the goals of the total library, rather than on the basis of the goals and needs of one's immediate work group. Administrative skills include planning, programming, and organizaing work; assigning the right tasks to the right people; giving people the right amount of responsibility and authority; inspecting and following up on the work; and coordinating the efforts and activities of different organizational members, levels, and departments.[7]

Tasks, people, and institutional functions and purposes must be the focus of educational programs if librarians are to be effective. Without a recognition of these three forces in curriculum design, well-qualified personnel may fall short of the demand.

THE SUPERVISORY SKILL-MIX

Theoretically, one may suggest a paradigm in which technical skills become less important and administrative skills more important for supervisors at each succeeding higher level in the organization, with human relations skills being about equally important for supervisors at all levels, but somewhat less crucial at the very top level. Table 2 presents schematically a conception of the relative importance of the three kinds of supervisor skills for the following four different levels of supervision:

1. **Highest Level Administrator**

   Description: Deciding on goals of the library, on changes in these goals, on the resources used to obtain these goals, and on the policies and strategies that are to goven the acquisition, use, and disposition of these resources.

   Activities: Establishing general goals; identifying environmental forces which define and limit library activities; becoming aware of the need to change; organizing for change; projecting future factors which define and limit library activities; evaluating, selecting, and deciding on alternatives; establishing specific plans of action; gaining approval of plans; implementing change through plans.

2. **Department Supervisor**

   Description: Assuring that resources (human, capital, natural, ideational, material) are obtained and used effectively and efficiently in the accomplishment of the library goals.

   Activities: Getting things done through people; coordinating techniques, materials, procedures, plans, people, capital, and facilities to facilitate flow of a particular required library function.

3. **Cataloger**

   Description: Under the supervision of the chief librarian, has charge of the cataloging and classification of books.

   Activities: Cataloging, classifying, and assigning subject headings; making master cards and adapting Library of Congress or other cards; keeping the shelf list; revising and supervising or handling processing details; developing the catalogs and cataloging procedures to meet the needs of the college; searching for catalog information; making recommendations and decisions in matters of cataloging policy; maintaining a manual of cataloging routines; keeping essential records and statistics; preparing reports and memoranda; and handling correspondence.[8]

4. **Catalog Library Clerk**

   Description: Under the supervision of the cataloger, has charge of the catalog and book-related processing.

   Activities: Typing and adapting Library of Congress cards from copy supplied; withdrawing cards from the catalog and shelf list; filing cards; distributing catalog cards received on order; shelf-listing; changing records for items added or withdrawn; operating mimeograph and other duplicating machines; marking books; bookplating; and other related processes.[9]

The relative importance of each kind of skill is likely to vary across library organizational levels. At the highest level, administrative skills are probably more important. At the lower level, catalog library clerk, programmed technical skills and human relations skills are the most important. For the

TABLE II
RELATIVE IMPORTANCE OF DIFFERENT SKILLS

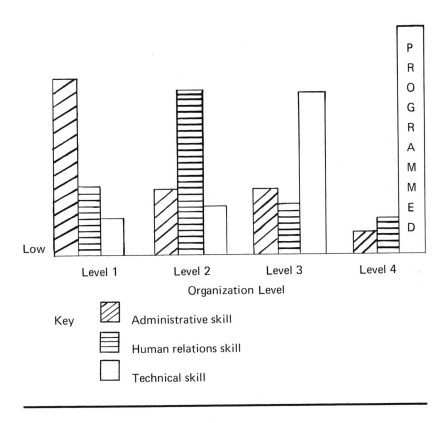

cataloger, level three, nonprogrammed technical skills and human relations skills are most important. At level two, the department supervisor, human relations skills are most important although technical know-how is vital. Skill-mix requirements will vary according to the development (age) of the library system, time dimension, and technology.

In conclusion, skill level development is as important to an organization as the development of library collections and capital. Qualified personnel are obviously essential to the health and life of the library.

To clarify the dynamics of BBPS, it seems wise to "walk through" the personnel process to apply behavioral-oriented activities in the library. The walk-through consists of a case study in Chapter V.

FOOTNOTES

[1] For supporting research on skill level mix in other fields, see Floyd Mann, "Toward An Understanding of the Leadership Role in Formal Organizations," in Robert Dubin and others, *Leadership and Productivity* (San Francisco: Chandler Publishing Company, 1965), pp. 69-76.

[2] A task is defined as an event or specified activity performed in relation to the tools, materials, equipment, and technology used in achieving organizational objectives.

[3] See Ad Hoc Recruitment Committee, "A Proposal for a School Library Manpower Project" (Chicago: American Association of School Librarians, 1967), p. 5.

[4] Herbert Simon, *The New Science of Management Decisions* (New York: Harper and Row, Inc., 1960), pp. 5-6.

[5] Basil S. Georgopoulos and Floyd C. Mann, "Supervisor and Administrative Behavior," in Robert A. Sutermeister, *People and Productivity,* 2d. ed. (New York: McGraw-Hill, 1969), pp. 381-82.

[6] *Ibid.,* pp. 382-83.

[7] *Ibid.,* p. 283.

[8] ALA Board on salaries, staff and tenure. Subcommittee on budgets, compensation and schemes of service . . . *Classification and Pay Plans for Libraries in Institutions of Higher Education,* Vol. II, Degree-conferring four-year institutions, 2d. ed. (Chicago: American Library Association, 1947), pp. 23-33.

[9] *Ibid.,* pp. 88-90.

BASIC REFERENCES

Dubin, Robert and others. *Leadership and Productivity* (San Francisco: Chandler Publishing Company, 1965).

French, Wendell. *The Personnel Management Process,* 2d. ed. (Boston: Houghton-Mifflin Company, 1970), pp. 477-538.

Georgopoulos, Basil and Floyd C. Mann, "Supervisor and Administrative Behavior," in *People and Productivity* by Robert A. Sutermeister (New York: McGraw-Hill, 1969), pp. 381-2.

Peter, Laurence J. and Raymond Hull. *Peter Principle* (New York: W. Morrow, 1969).

CHAPTER V

BEHAVIORAL ENVIRONMENT:
PRAIRIE STATE COLLEGE LIBRARY

Prairie State College is a state, tax-supported liberal and applied arts college, established and maintained by the state to serve its residents, particularly from the western part of the state, in all those ways for which such an institution is authorized, prepared, and equipped to be of service. The college consists of twenty-four departments which offer Bachelor of Arts and Bachelor of Science degrees. In addition, twenty-one departments in the college offer degrees on the master's level. The college's enrollment in the academic year of 1962-63 was approximately 3700 full-time students.

"The library of Prairie State College is considered the 'hub' of a scholarly wheel from which academic spokes radiate in all directions. It is the center of learning activities and, as such, is the most important intellectual resource of the academic community."[1]

In the academic year of 1962-63, according to the U.S. Department of Education's Biennial Report, Eberhard Library was considered to be a medium-size college collection of research materials. The director, Fred K. Pauly, was responsible to the president, N. D. Hoyt. Although the financial and administrative activities of the college were handled by administrative departments, the library—through the efforts of the director—conducted its academic transactions as a separate department of the college. Certain state requirements, however, required some of the library transactions to be funneled through the administrative offices (see *Excerpts from Acquisitions Manual,* pp. 77-79).

The president delegated authority for hiring, purchasing, and planning activities vital to effective library service to the director of libraries. He expressed his feeling concerning his allocation of responsibility to the director by stating, "The college has grown to such a size during the past decade that I cannot properly handle or check the various responsibilities and activities of each department on campus. Therefore, I have given Fred an open hand concerning the library's operation."

In a conversation between two professional librarians concerning the president's attitude toward the library, the following statement was made: "The only time the prexy has ever been in the library since I began work here in 1954 was when he posed for a news photograph with Mr. M. B. King who had donated some rare manuscripts to the library. I don't believe he has been in the library building since then, 1958."

PRAIRIE STATE COLLEGE LIBRARY

Because of the extremely crowded conditions of the library building and the lack of complete air-conditioning throughout, physical working conditions for those on the staff were not considered extremely favorable. Air-conditioning was important, especially during the hot summer months. Some sections of the library, however, did have air-conditioning—the director's office, the main reading room, the tehcnical service department, and the small reading and service area of the government documents section. It was the casewriter's opinion that the poor physical working conditions in the library were only of minor consequence upon the morale of the library staff. They seemed to be offset by the immediate planning of a new completely air-conditioned building. Construction of the new facilities was to begin in July of 1965.

In September of 1962, the library employed eight professional librarians, five full-time civil service clerical workers, and approximately seventy-five part-time student assistants. The professional librarians, including Mr. Pauly, would have preferred more full-time clerical workers rather than the large number of part-time student assistants. In this respect they could not influence the president to discard his policy for filling positions with numerous part-time students rather than a few full-time employees.

Exhibit 1 shows the organizational structure of the library as approved by the director of libraries in January of 1963.

Salaries of the professional librarians were slightly below the average for other staff members of the college. Salary increases and academic promotions were based solely upon the recommendations made by the director to the president. The director of libraries was employed on a twelve-month basis. All other professional librarians were hired on an eleven-month contract. A professional librarian with faculty status and academic rank at Prairie State was required to have a master's degree in Library Science from an accredited American Library Association graduate library school.

Civil service personnel were salaried by the rates and schedules developed by the State Civil Service Agency. The salary increases were based upon the agency's schedules and thus resulted in various incomes among the five members. Student assistants received seventy-five cents per hour which was the standard part-time student rate on campus.

The professional librarians were not required to use a time clock or adhere strictly to an exact work schedule. The director did request that each person submit to him his planned schedule for each academic quarter. This schedule was to include lunch hours, office hours, evening reference duty assignments, and classroom schedules. Several members of the staff taught one or two courses per quarter in the library science program. In addition to maintaining a liberal working schedule, the director was known to be very sympathetic toward staff requests for absenteeism from their departments for various personal and professional reasons. Mr. Pauly told his assistant that he thought professional librarians should not have to use the time clock or

EXHIBIT 1. PRAIRIE STATE COLLEGE EBERHARD LIBRARY — ORGANIZATIONAL CHART

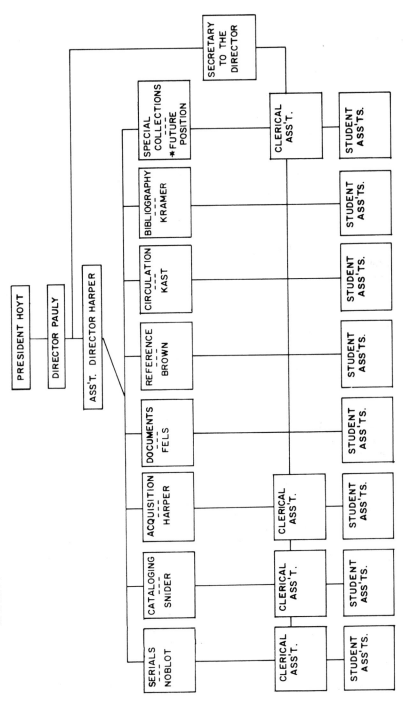

stick to a rigid schedule, but he did think that they should leave word with one of their assistants when it was going to be necessary for them to be out of the library. To illustrate this philosophy, Mr. Pauly—after being unable to locate Mr. Brown—circulated a memorandum to all librarians (see Exhibit 2).

EXHIBIT 2

Memorandum to Librarians

October 14, 1963

During the past few weeks, professional librarians have been away from the library and have not left word concerning their whereabouts. If you prefer to be allowed to leave the library at your discretion, I suggest you either leave word with one of your assistants or with Mrs. Undermeyer. If you do not wish to comply with this request, I suggest that you make out a Request for Absence at the President's office.

Fred K. Pauly

FKP:pu

The professional librarians and faculty members followed the same holiday and quarter-recess schedule. Professional librarians worked a forty-hour week. If a librarian were to work on Saturday or on a week night he was given equal time off during regular work days to compensate.

The civil service workers were on duty eight hours daily, five days a week. They received one day a month vacation and seven days' sick leave per year. With the exception of the director's secretary, all civil service employees were to follow the coffee-break schedule that he personally developed for each academic year. The schedule indicated that only one civil service girl would be gone from the library at one time. His reasons concerning this action were two-fold: First, someone must be on duty to answer the telephone and to receive visitors wishing to see various staff members. The second reason stems from a comment he made to his assistant in 1962, "It's all right for the civil service girls to talk about me, but I prefer that they not do it on my time."

It was not uncommon for civil service workers and student assistants to receive written communications on occasion stating that there was unnecessary talking among civil service and student assistants during work hours and that such action should be discontinued at once (see Exhibit 3). The director mentioned to one of the professional staff members that his philosophy concerning the administration of non-professionals was, "If you are going to get the most out of your personnel, you have to keep after them

all the time, allow no visiting, and see that they are concerned with nothing
but the immediate task."

EXHIBIT 3

Memorandum to Non-Professional Employees

To all non-professional employees:

I have received complaints that there is too much noise in staff work
areas. This should be discontinued at once. If your supervisor cannot
keep you busy, let me know. I have plenty of work to keep a hundred
people busy. Like the old sailor once said, "Shape up or ship out."

Fred K. Pauly
Director

Civil service workers were assigned to various departments on campus by
a member of the business office staff. The director of the library had the right
to interview all candidates available prior to their hiring. Once they were
assigned to the library, the director reported their progress to the officer in
charge of civil service employees concerning such matters as sick leave,
vacations, salary, and annual progress reports. This was done even though
the civil service worker was assigned to a particular librarian for supervision.
Although Mr. Pauly made the professional librarians responsible for assigning
tasks and supervising civil service employees, he preferred to be responsible
for recommending them for pay raises and promotions. During the two-year
period in which the casewriter was employed at Prairie State, Mr. Pauly did
not consult any professional librarian concerning recommendations for civil
service employees. This led to several conflicts for which one is cited as an
illustration.

Mrs. Toody, a clerical worker for the acquisitions department, approached
Mr. Harper in late January of 1963 concerning a special pay increase for all
state civil service employees. This pay increase was to be put into effect
February 1, 1963. Mrs. Toody explained that she represented all five civil
service workers in the library concerning this matter. She wished to know if
Harper could find out if the five workers would receive the pay increase. It
was their understanding that the supervisors were to recommend each civil
service worker in order that they be eligible for the salary increase.

Harper agreed to contact Mr. Little of the business office. At the time
of the inquiry Mr. Harper was told that such recommendations were due on
Friday of the previous week. In addition, he was told that only one girl, Mrs.
Snider's secretary, had been recommended by Mr. Pauly. Harper then asked if

it was possible for him to recommend the civil service employee under his supervision. Mr. Little replied that only Mr. Pauly could make such a recommendation.

Harper related this information to Mrs. Toody. He volunteered to approach Mr. Pauly concerning such action, but Mrs. Toody preferred that he not mention it. Harper did see Mrs. Snider about the situation, but learned that she, too, knew nothing about recommending any civil service employee for a salary increase.

The professional librarians were assigned to various staff positions by the director. These departments were typical of the functional library organization (see Exhibit 1). Each professional librarian was responsible for the activities assigned to his department. The various functions of the departments were modified from time to time by Mr. Pauly. The assigning of a new task without prior notification was not uncommon nor was the switching of tasks from department to department. This procedure was noted on several occasions, two of which will be cited here. On one occasion a staff member assigned to the bibliography section returned from summer vacation to find that her desk had been moved to another area of the library and her assignment changed from that of bibliography librarian to reference librarian. No prior notice had been given to her. The director, who worked during August, had made the adjustments during her absence.

On a second occasion a professional staff member, during a staff meeting prior to the August 1963 vacation, asked the director, "Are there going to be changes in either our assignments or work areas during August? I spent September of last year searching for my materials. I thought I would be prepared this year." Mr. Pauly replied that he did not plan any changes because of the crowded conditions of the library.

Although there were no formal written policies concerning librarian's and other members of the library staff's function and behavior, Mr. Pauly issued memoranda to this effect at various times. Usually these followed an action by a staff member which was considered unwarranted by the director. Such an example is shown in Exhibit 4. Even though the note was directed to one particular individual, copies were always circulated to all librarians. As no verbal communication concerning the matter was ever brought to the attention of the specific offender, librarians were sometimes in doubt as to who or what was the cause of the policy.

During the academic year of 1962-63, only two staff meetings were held to discuss library and teaching activities. In the academic year of 1963-64, regular weekly staff meetings were scheduled. These were the result of the many complaints by staff members concerning the feeling that they were not informed on all activities of the library. Oftentimes librarians felt embarrassed when a situation concerning the library procedures developed and they were unable to cope with the problem because of a lack of information. As example of such lack of communication was illustrated when two professional librarians discovered that *Southwestern Notes* was initiated and issued as an Eberhard Library publication. The librarians discovered this fact approximately one and half years after it was first circulated on a quarterly basis.

EXHIBIT 4

Memorandum to the Library Staff

April 8, 1964

Because of misuse of authority concerning budget and mails, beginning today, April 8, 1964, all out-going mail will be placed in the basket provided. This basket is located just inside the Library office door. All incoming mail will be delivered to the Library office and distribution will be made from there.

Any mass distribution through the mail (on campus or off) involving library materials and funds will be cleared with me before funds will be approved.

Fred K. Pauly

FKP:vmh

The weekly staff meetings continued for six weeks and then ceased except for a special meeting or two. The first meetings included a presentation by each department head concerning his department's routine activities of the present and past year.

PERSONAL BACKGROUNDS

Fred K. Pauly was employed as director of the library at Prairie State by President N. D. Hoyt in 1956. Mr. Pauly was the first director to be hired since 1954. Miss Jean Fels had been acting librarian since the death of Henry Miles[2] in 1954. Miss Fels had been at Prairie State since 1945. She declined the directorship when it was offered, but remained on the staff as the documents librarian.

Mr. Pauly was the fourth male librarian to be hired in the college's entire history. Hal Brown, a present staff member, who was hired in 1954 was the third. Mr. Pauly came to Prairie State from a one-year tenure at Timken, Colorado where he had been a librarian at the Veterans Administration Hospital library. This fact was taken from Pauly's record in the president's office. It contradicted a remark Pauly had made to his assistant and two State University library directors during a conference held in Harris. At that time Pauly stated that he was employed as director of libraries for the Veterans Administration and worked in Denver, Colorado.

Timken was a small town in Eastern Colorado where a small veterans' hospital was located. Mr. Pauly had taken the position upon graduation from library school at Illinois, because of its salary. He resigned a year later as he did not like the formal organization and procedures that were to be adhered to under such a federal library system. He complained of his inability to do anything on his own. He preferred a job where he was free to set policy and procedures. (This latter information was taken from a conversation between the casewriter and Mr. Pauly.)

In 1962, Fred was thirty-eight years old. Prior to his completion of graduate work, he spent one year as a teacher-librarian at Liota High School, a small high school in Eastern Oklahoma. After what he described as a "poor experience," he went back to Illinois to finish his library program which he had started the previous summer. Pauly finished his undergraduate degree at Oklahoma Wesleyan in 1953.

Pauly's wife was a registered nurse at the Harris Memorial Hospital and had been since their arrival in 1956. At present she was the night supervisor. The Paulys had two sons, ages 14 and 11. It was mostly through Mrs. Pauly's employment that Fred had been able to attend college after a ten-year tour in the Navy.

Pauly was one of twelve of the one-hundred eighty-seven full-time faculty and staff members at Prairie State who held a membership in the newly formed Pine Crest Country Club. The exclusive club was made up largely of the doctors, lawyers, and elite businessmen of the community.

Mr. Pauly submitted a fee which allowed him to be listed in the biography, *Who's Who in American Education.* Pauly preferred to keep his name in front of those with whom he had contact. He carried and distributed a specially designed call card with his name and position inscribed on it. He used this card even though the college issued form cards for each of its members. Pauly also was the first State Library Association president who had special envelopes with his name inscribed below the address of the organization. This procedure was followed even though an abundance of printed envelopes with the association's name was available. Prior to 1962, he also distributed to all professional librarians a form letter with his name pretyped in the closing. The librarians were requested to use these forms whenever they requisitioned materials for the collection. As a result, the bulk of incoming library materials were addressed to Mr. Pauly.

Fred Pauly was a very active committee member, both concerning campus and professional activities. During the 1962-63 academic year, he was a member of three major committees on campus, the Governor's library committee, and the State Library Committee.

Committee work usually required a great deal of Pauly's working hours. While at the library during his regular hours, Pauly performed the following duties every day regardless of what other matters arose: (1) sorting incoming mail, (2) sorting mail and materials for distribution to the various departments of the library, (3) pleasure and professional reading, and (4) conferring with the professional staff concerning daily library problems.

President N. D. Hoyt made the following statement to the casewriter concerning Mr. Pauly: "When Fred took over in 1956, the library situation was critical. Henry Miles, bless his ole soul, was quite a person and a scholar, but he didn't give the library the leadership it needed to be the center of campus scholarship. Today the picture is much brighter and I give Fred all the credit for the marked improvement."

Miss Jean Fels was the senior member of the professional library staff. She had been in the documents department since joining the staff. She developed the collection and in some aspects the classification system used. It was apparent to all professional librarians that Miss Fels took great pride in developing the documents collection. Mr. Pauly made some minor changes in procedures developed by Miss Fels, but not all that he would have preferred. He once made the following statement to the casewriter regarding the documents collection and Miss Fels: "I think that much of the material in the documents collection is lost, because of the lack of bibliographic control, but I can't convince Jean to make the changes. Some day though, I'm going up there and pull a lot of the historical materials and get them where they belong."

Hal Brown, age 35, was the reference librarian. He had been employed prior to Pauly. He had served as circulation librarian for some time before Pauly changed him to his present position. Brown and his wife purchased their home in 1958. They were active in many faculty activities. As Mr. Brown was hired at a lower salary than the present starting salary for beginning librarians and his annual salary increases were not large, it was necessary for his family to "live from paycheck to paycheck." Hal was a member of the same supper club as Pauly (not to be confused with the country club) and had on occasion been appointed to various library committees by Pauly. Mr. Brown summarized his relationship with Pauly by stating, "Bette and I have had some of the best times ever at the boss', but as far as running the library—I'm not at all impressed. Ever since that first meeting he had with the staff back in '56 I haven't had any respect for him as an administrator. He told us, 'If you don't like the way I do—or am going to run things here— you can all quit.' This meeting took place only two days after Pauly arrived in Harris." In 1962 Hal Brown was the president of the Prairie State Faculty Association, the incoming president of the Faculty Men's Club, and chairman of the local chapter of the State School Librarians Association. He also was an active member in many professional and educational associations and took part in various campus committees.

Mabel Snider, head of cataloging, was the first of the present library staff to be hired by Mr. Pauly. She came directly from a graduate library school. Mabel was 52 and a widow. She was considered by all professional librarians to be the closest personal friend of Mr. Pauly. Part of this relationship was due to the personal friendship between Mrs. Pauly and Mrs. Snider. When Mrs. Snider encountered a problem, she went to Pauly for advice. Although not a member of the Country Club, she did have a golf membership which entitled her access to the eating and golf facilities.

Mabel told the casewriter that she came to Prairie State because Pauly had promised her the position of Head of Technical Processes, a position she later found out never did, or never would, exist. She told the casewriter during a dispute over policy, "I don't make decisions, I just put in my time and receive a salary in return."

Mrs. Snider was Mr. Pauly's most frequent visitor during the working hours. These visits were both of personal and professional nature. Although she had on numerous occasions suggested some possible changes in cataloging processes, no major changes had been made since 1958. As a result, when she encountered a problem not covered by a policy, she immediately sought Pauly's advice. This was not limited to library matters alone. She also conferred with him on the kind of new car she should purchase, whether she should put a basement under her home, what type of lawn she should plant, and whether she should attend various professional conferences. These facts were discovered by the casewriter during trips and discussions among the three. Mrs. Snider had the following comment for the casewriter concerning Mr. Pauly: "Fred has done quite a lot for this library. You should have been here in 1958. Fred may be difficult at times, but he does get things done. He has an abundance of nervous energy."

Miss Nancy Kramer and Miss Ruby Noblot were additions to the staff in 1961. Both were single and approximately thirty-five years old. Miss Kramer was the full-time instructor in library science and also served as bibliography librarian. During her first two years at Prairie State she encountered considerable trouble concerning the controversial Methods of Research course which was required for all graduate students. The course was required for all students prior to Pauly's employment at Prairie State, but had been adapted to Mr. Pauly's philosophy of how such a course should be handled. It appeared to the casewriter that many of the problems concerning the course disappeared during Miss Kramer's third year. It was at this time that she began to change the course content and methods to more closely meet the desires of the graduate school program committee.

Ruby Noblot was twenty-eight when she entered college. She worked as a student assistant while attending P.S.C. Through the encouragement of Mr. Pauly, she completed requirements for a graduate degree in librarianship. Ruby was a person who made it a matter of principle to be at work precisely at 8:30 and leave precisely at 5:00. She often worked on Saturdays to see if she could clear some of the incoming materials for processing to the stack areas. In addition to handling regular serial and subscription items, she was in charge of preparing bindery materials, serial gifts and exchanges, and detail work for the State Union List of Serials project. This was a project of the five state institutions of higher learning.

As it was Pauly's policy to add all serial items that were not presently in the library, regardless of whether they met the needs of the college, Miss Noblot's area was constantly overflowing with stacks of unprocessed materials. Every possible space in the serials area was filled with miscellaneous magazines, newspapers, and serial items. This included all shelf space, areas beneath tables and files, and unused space in other technical process areas. Much of the difficulty arose from the policy that detailed classification and cataloging should be completed on all materials before sending them to respective stack areas. As Miss Noblot was the only one in the department who could do this type of bibliographic searching, the process was quite time consuming. Handling these unprocessed materials was only a small portion of Miss Noblot's departmental functions. The processing of current materials required seventy-five per cent of her total working hours.

On a Saturday in the early spring of 1963, Mr. Pauly, Mrs. Snider, and two student assistants began to process the numerous miscellaneous materials in an effort to clear the material from the technical processing area. Mrs. Snider told the casewriter she was on duty when Mr. Pauly arrived unexpectedly that Saturday morning. About an hour after he arrived, Mrs. Snider stated that he came out of his office and told her that he had decided to call two student assistants to help clear some serial items. The four people worked all day Saturday and Sunday doing temporary processing of all available miscellaneous items. On Sunday evening the project was completed. It was learned later that Mr. Pauly had come to the library for the purpose of handling some scheduled library tours for visiting high school honor students.

On the following Monday at 8:30 a.m., Miss Noblot walked into the serials area and was completely surprised and astonished to find that the bulk of the materials was gone. Later, Mr. Pauly called her into his office to tell her of the weekend activities.

Mrs. Snider told the casewriter about a week later that Miss Noblot had been in tears when she met her and Miss Kramer for their usual coffee break. Miss Noblot was upset by the fact that she had not been contacted concerning the move, nor approached about being able to make only temporary cards for the materials.

Mr. Pauly told the casewriter during a conversation that took place while the two were traveling to a conference that, "The library profession needs conscientious and shy people such as Ruby. I believe that the profession benefits from the workmanship given by these people behind the scenes as well as the public service and public relations personnel."

A seventh member of the staff was Jerry Kast. He was a nonprofessional librarian when hired in 1961. Mr. Kast, who had just received his B. A. from Prairie State, was married. He was about thirty years old. He was given the position at P.S.C. with the understanding that he would attend graduate library school during three consecutive summers in order to receive his librarianship degree. After receiving the degree, he promised Mr. Pauly that he would stay at P. S. C. for at least two additional years. Kast received a salary substantially less than any of the other professional librarians, but was promised by Mr. Pauly that he would get a large increase upon completion of his graduate degree. He also had begun study toward a graduate degree in sociology at Prairie State. Faculty and staff members were allowed to take a maximum of three hours per semester during regular academic sessions. Hal Brown had recently received a second M.A. in history by taking courses under this arrangement.

Kast was always the first to arrive at the library in the mornings. Although his quitting hours were scheduled at 5:00 p.m. each day, he usually worked until 6:00 p.m. It was not unusual for him to work several hours on each Saturday and on evenings when he was not scheduled. Kast told the casewriter in May of 1963 that he had "finally been able to cut his work week from one of sixty hours to one of fifty."

In the casewriter's opinion, Kast was a victim of at least two circumstances that made his position the target of Mr. Pauly's criticism. First, he was responsible for the regular stack area where 150,000 volumes were stored, where 80,000 volumes, according to present library standards, should have been the top limit. Second, he was an inexperienced supervisor of an area where much leg work was required during all hours of the day and evening. Because of space limitations, a "closed shelf" circulation system was used at Eberhard Library. The circulation area was the least desirable to student workers because of the amount of time spent running up and down stairs and because of the lack of air-conditioning. Kast was also in charge of the audio-visual department of the library. The department was established to meet the needs of the college and high schools in the surrounding areas. Many of ther materials were, as a rule, worn and dated. During the 1961-62 academic session only two films were purchased, both replacements of titles already in the collection. Mr. Kast turned in numerous requests to Mr. Pauly for both new titles and replacements, but the requests were never processed.

Pauly was responsible for the audio-visual services being in the library. Previously the service had been handled by the education department. Under the old arrangement a separate budget for both materials and equipment had been available. At present, the library equipment fund and materials fund were used to purchase the audio-visual inventory. Pauly secured the service as an addition to the library program in 1959 by showing the Council of Division Chairmen that the audio-visual program could be more effectively maintained if it were a part of the library's program.

THOUGHT QUESTIONS (PART 1)

1. What assumptions does President Hoyt make concerning Mr. Pauly's leadership ability?

2. What personnel assumptions does Mr. Pauly make in regard to civil service employees?

   In answering this question, give consideration to:
   a. The use of professional librarians to assist in selection and evaluation of civil service employees.
   b. The justification of each policy including:
      1) use of the time clock
      2) conversation during working hours
      3) coffee break schedules

3. Do you agree with the action taken by Mr. Pauly in *a* and *b* above?

4. Do you agree with the approach to supervision of professional librarians as developed by Mr. Pauly? Why or why not?

5. Determine the potential sources of job satisfaction for Mr. Pauly, Mr. Brown, Mr. Kast, and Mrs. Snider.

6. How would you justify Mr. Pauly's leadership behavior as exhibited in managing professional librarians as opposed to managing clerical assistants?

7. What part does "status" play in job satisfaction of all employees of Eberhard Library? Why was it important?

8. What was the primary source of "status" for Mr. Brown and Mr. Pauly?

9. What possible justification could Mr. Pauly have for using the procedure that was followed in clearing the serials department of unprocessed materials? Do you agree with the action taken by Mr. Pauly? What were the alternatives?

A NEW STAFF MEMBER

President Hoyt authorized Pauly to hire one additional professional librarian for the 1962-63 academic year. Pauly reported to the president that he would seek the services of an acquisitions librarian. The acquisitions procedures were at the present time handled by Mr. Pauly, one civil service worker, and several student assistants.

Pauly contacted each of the thirty-two accredited library schools concerning the position. This was done in June of 1962. In August, he contacted the director of a school of librarianship concerning a possible date for him to be on campus in mid-August to interview possible candidates. Because the number of library positions available greatly outnumbered the number of library school graduates, Pauly anticipated some difficulty in securing the person he wanted to handle the position. He told Dick Steen, a senior at P.S.C. who planned on attending graduate library school, that he wanted a young man who had approximately the same philosophy as his to handle the acquisitions and assistant director position.

On August 10, 1962, Dick Harper, a 26-year-old graduate student in his third summer, met with Pauly. Harper at that time had met all the requirements for his degree except a two and one-half quarter-hour research paper requirement and an additional six hours of electives outside the school of librarianship curriculum. He and his wife both expected to stay and receive their degrees in December.

The Harpers had three years of public school teacher-librarian experience. They had met state library certification requirements prior to entering the university. Dick had majored in business administration as an undergraduate. As a result of his combined experience and academic background, he met all existing requirements for the position, except the librarianship degree.

The interview between Pauly and Harper covered topics concerning personal backgrounds, reading interests, academic backgrounds, Harper's graduation date, the position offered, background material on Prairie State, economic and geographic conditions of the Harris area, academic goals of Harper, and job possibilities for Mrs. Harper.

The bulk of the ending conversation follows:

Pauly: From what you have said, you could be available in September if Dr. Short could arrange for you to complete your research in Harris and take a graduate course at P.S. C. which would meet your degree requirements.

Harper: Yes, that is correct, except that my graduation date would be delayed until March 15, 1963. I would actually finish my work in December, but I would have to wait until March 15 to receive the degree.

Pauly: If you're interested in the job of acquisitions librarian and assistant director of Eberhard Library, I would prefer that you take the job in September. You would gain valuable experience, earn a professional librarian's salary, and be of value to P.S.C. while still completing your degree requirements. The main reason for my suggesting this is that I have a possibility of losing the position if I cannot fill it by September. You see, I compete with the remainder of the divisions at P.S. C. for new positions. If I fail to fill the position, another division would be given the opportunity to expand its staff.

Harper: I believe that with your assistance I could arrange to work out the details with Dr. Short, but I'm still wondering about employment for my wife.

Pauly: I'm sure I can find her a job when I return to Harris. The public library is thinking of hiring a new director and the state library is planning to hire a consultant for the western portion of the state. I'm in a position to help her get either of the jobs. There is also the possibility that one of the three high schools will be seeking a librarian. As I stated before, she is always assured of all summer employment at P.S.C. by handling the summer librarian-ship courses and workshops. The state allows us to hire spouses for special occasions even though it has a nepotism law.

Harper: That sounds promising. I'll talk it over with Mary. You stated before that upon receiving my M.L.S. I could expect a raise in salary and assume the assistant directorship.

Pauly: That's correct. As I stated before, I'm looking for a person who will work closely with me and who has the ability to study, evaluate, and reorganize the acquisitions department. You'll have a chance to work on library committees with me, write articles and procedures for the library, set policy, and supervise other librarians and employees. Since I'll have to devote a great deal of my time working on the new library plans, you'll be able to get a wealth of experience. From what you have told me, this is the type of position you seem to be seeking.

Harper: It certainly has possibilities. The academic surroundings, the challenges of the position, and the experience I could gain seems

46

very enticing. I'm partial to the mountain country and surroundings, but would be willing to live in the Southwest if the advantages of working there are vital to my attainment of future goals.

Pauly: I certainly hope you will give serious thought to this offer. With your permission, I'll speak to Dr. Short, and when I return to Harris, I'll contact President Hoyt. If all can be worked out, I'll contact you in the very near future.

Harper: You have my permission to consider me for the position. As this is an important decision for me, I'll talk it over with my wife. If details can be worked out for both Mary and me, I'll be happy to answer immediately any correspondence I receive from you or President Hoyt.

Pauly: Excellent. I'm sure you'll hear from me next week.

On the following Tuesday, Mr. Harper received a letter from President Hoyt acknowledging Mr. Pauly's offer. The letter was to be considered as a contract for the year 1962-63, if accepted. After consulting Dr. Short, Jerry Kast, a former P.S.C. librarian, a former P.S.C. graduate, and written materials concerning the college and community, Mr. Harper decided to accept the position. During the remainder of the time before going to Harris, Harper had numerous telephone contacts with Pauly concerning various matters of hoursing, course work, assignments, and so forth.

On August 28, 1962, Harper and his wife arrived in Harris. Several days later Mr. Harper met with Mr. Pauly. During this meeting, Pauly told Harper that he had contacted Miss Georgia Fish, acting state librarian, concerning a meeting he had arranged during the two-day State Library Association conference that was to be held in October. He told Harper that Miss Fish would discuss with Mrs. Harper the job opening he had mentioned earlier.

On September 4, 1962, Harper met for the first time with the entire library staff. Pauly introduced Harper as the new acquisitions librarian, but no mention was made of the assistant directorship. Later during the day he told Harper that he previously mentioned to the entire staff that Harper was to be in charge when he was out of town.

Harper took part in the two-day faculty workshop which preceded the beginning of the fall semester. At this time he learned through meetings with faculty members that the existing problems of the library related to space, insufficient funds for materials, and a lack of direct communication between library and faculty members. The communication problem, as expressed by the library study committee, was directed at the library's failure to respond to faculty requests for new materials. A one-year backlog of filing in the main library catalog made this type of communication a necessity.

REQUIRED BEHAVIOR

The acquistions department was located in the main technical processing area. Pauly directed Harper to arrange his work area immediately adjacent to

47

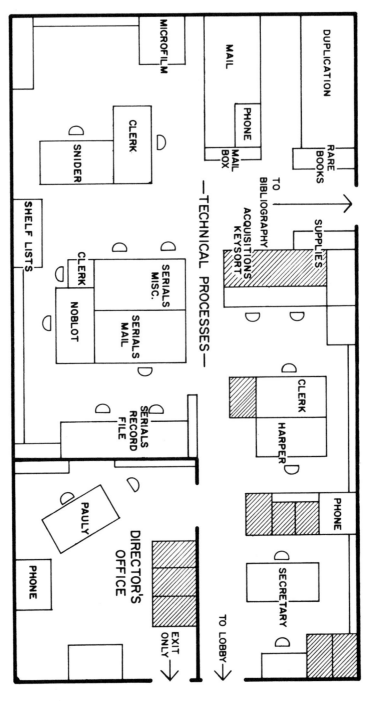

Exhibit 5

4 DRAWER AND OTHER 5' FILES

Pauly's office so that Harper would be available for consultation (see Exhibit 5). Harper's civil service worker had been employed only three weeks prior to September 1, and the student assistants to be assigned would be new to the department. This was done so that Mr. Harper could train his personnel exactly as he saw necessary.

While rearranging his work area Harper was directed to put files between his area and Pauly's secretary's area as no partitions separated the technical processing department. Pauly's reason for the needed separation was, "I want the two civil service girls to know where their work areas are. By separating them, we eliminate any possible interaction between them except on matters where job requirements make it necessary."

The two other technical processes departments located in the area were also separated by files, tables, and so forth (see Exhibit 5), and interaction between workers seemed difficult. Harper noticed that memoranda were posted on the bulletin boards telling civil service workers that talking was to be held to a minimum at all times (see Exhibit 3). Harper noticed that all talking seemed to cease immediately when Pauly came into the processing area.

This type of conduct continued as long as Pauly was present. During the first month of Harper's employment, it was noticeable that his own presence created the same quiet effect. It wasn't until late in October after Harper had been able to express his attitudes concerning informal interaction being necessary for a good working environment that his presence did not cause silence.

Upon returning to his office unexpectedly at a time when Mr. Pauly was out, Harper noticed that all workers were clustered in a group, each performing some task which did not limit them to one specific area. When one of the workers saw Harper approaching from the lobby, she warned the others. Everyone returned to their respective areas. Harper noticed the reactions and stated, "Don't let me interrupt your discussion or work. As long as the work that is assigned is finished on schedule, I don't care if you visit one another. I do think that you should not visit when Mr. Pauly is in the office though. Mr. Pauly and I don't agree on interaction between employees during work hours."

Harper spent much of his time during the next three months conferring with Pauly. New procedures were being worked out, each being reviewed before implementation. A compromise on the part of both men was necessary in the reorganization of the acquisitions department. Harper found that the present acquisitions procedures and methods had to be used even though they were not as effective as those he preferred.

In the early months of Harper's employment, he seldom had coffee with any of the staff members. Pauly drank coffee in his office as coffee was available for those who cared to indulge. Mrs. Snider also drank coffee at the library, but went to the Memorial Union for morning and afternoon coffee breaks. All of the faculty members usually had coffee at the Union and librarians visited with them during these breaks.

Hal Brown and Jerry Kast asked Harper to go to coffee, but Harper seldom accompanied them. Harper did on occasion go to coffee with Pauly, but he usually accompanied a faculty member whom he had contacted concerning future purchase of materials in special subject areas.

Beginning in late October, Pauly and Harper went to various library conferences each month. They were gone about twice a month. Pauly, as president of the State Library Association, had selected Harper to be publicity director for the Association and a member of the executive council; both were members of the State Library Council.

During these trips which were usually two or three days in length, Harper and Pauly would talk of plans for future growth of the library and of personal matters. Mr. Harper and Mr. Pauly continued a close relationship at the library. New plans continued to be implemented and reviewed each day. As Harper gained experience, more duties were given to him, but usually decisions were made by Pauly. Harper's role was that of suggesting new plans for the overall library program. The responsibility for book and material selection for the library had been delegated to Harper. He was under the impression that he was to be doing all purchasing of materials and issuing vouchers for payment. It wasn't until February of 1963 that Pauly stated, "I've made special deals with G. Frank Booksellers and King Books so I'll handle all orders and payments for these two dealers. You won't have to make any records for these materials unless I give you specific instructions."

Seldom did any occasion cause friction between the two men until April 24, 1963, when Dr. J. P. Orb of the Educational Field Services of the college made a visit to Harper's office. Orb was director of the Field Service Committee which made contracts with various school systems throughout the western section of the state. The contracts included arrangements for study and evaluation of the complete educational programs of public school systems. Orb had visited the library in March. At that time Pauly was away on personal business. On that occasion Orb had come to get a library evaluation report that was to be used in a current study. Upon being told by Pauly's secretary that Mr. Pauly hadn't made the report, Orb—knowing of Harper's past experience—approached Harper concerning his needs. Three weeks later, Harper had finished a forty-page report that Orb used in his publication. Today's visit by Orb was made to inquire if Harper would make a similar report for two other schools.

Pauly was present when Orb arrived. Because of Pauly's three past failures to make reports for him, Orb decided to work directly with Harper. Orb discussed the matter with Harper at Harper's desk. During their conversation, Pauly came out of his office and began to sort mail near Harper's area.

After Orb had gone from the library, Pauly called Harper to his office where he pointed out a few minor errors made by acquisition assistants. These errors were made in processing gift items that Harper had not processed. He also directed Harper to see that some of the talking among workers in the technical processes area was controlled, as he believed it was getting out of hand. During the remainder of the week Pauly and Harper held no other conferences on either library or personal matters.

Another incident arose in late April that also put a strain on the relationship between Pauly and Harper. This arose on a Thursday morning when Harper and Dick Steen were having a discussion concerning possibilities for speeding the cataloging process, particularly the process of securing cards prior to the arrival of books at a library. Harper, who was supervising an independent study course for Steen, pointed out the various alternatives available. Toward the end of the conversation, Mrs. Snider came into the room and began doing some cataloging. Harper left the room when Steen's questions had been answered and went out for lunch. He told Steen that if he had further questions concerning the problem he would be in his office about 4 p.m.

That afternoon, Harper returned to his office where he found Pauly and Snider discussing multilith card reproduction. The conference was being held in the corner of the technical processes area. When Pauly passed Harper's desk, Harper—who had not seen Pauly at all during the day—greeted him. Pauly gave no return greeting and went directly to his office and then left for the evening.

The following morning Harper visited Pauly concerning procedure changes in the acquisitions department. At the end of the conversation, Pauly made the following statement: "I'll think about this material and give you an answer soon. One thing I do know, though—we're not going to order catalog cards from the Library of Congress." (This is one of the alternatives a library has in securing cards for its card catalog. At that time, Eberhard Library was using a photographic method initiated by Pauly which was proving unsatisfactory. The multilith method mentioned above was another alternative.) The conversation continued:

Harper: Did someone say that we were going to do that?

Pauly: Apparently you and Dick Steen seem to think so.

Harper: Who told you that?

Pauly: Dick was in yesterday afternoon and mentioned it to me.

Harper: When did he say I made such a suggestion? I've seen Dick only once this week, and our conversation wasn't concerned with our catalog card reproduction process.

Pauly: According to Dick it was.

Harper: Dick must have his signals crossed. I think I'll go see him right now.

Pauly: No need to, I've forgotten the misunderstanding already. Besides, I contacted the printing office yesterday, and on Monday we are going to start using the multilith process on an experimental basis. The photographing system isn't working out as well as I thought it would when I purchased the microfilming equipment. Next time, however, please don't discuss library policy with our student assistants.

The conversation ended when Pauly left his office to go to lunch.

That afternoon Harper met Steen as the latter was coming into the library. Harper approached Steen concerning Pauly's insinuations. To this

Steen replied, "That damn liar; I haven't been to see him since last week. After you left yesterday Mrs. Snider and I talked concerning out general discussion of cataloging procedures. Apparently, from her conversation, she had been listening to us. She disagreed with you on certain issues, but I think it was clear that we weren't talking about the system in Eberhard Library. I bet she was the one who saw Pauly. I think she's out to get you. She resents your being the assistant director."

Harper: This isn't the first time something like this has happened. From now on, Dick, let's keep our personal conversations to ourselves.

Steen: I'm sure sorry if I'm the cause of friction between you and Pauly. Besides, I've got troubles of my own—my wife found out today that we are going to have a second child next fall. It looks as if I'll have to skip graduate school and find a job outside the library profession.

Harper: I hate to see you get out of the field, Dick. Are you sure you can't go on to school?

Steen: I could, for one quarter, but that's all we can afford.

Harper: If you can go for one quarter at State University, I think I can help you. Dr. Lowe of Eastern State College has had two positions open for two years and said that he is going to lose them if he doesn't fill them this spring. Rather than lose the positions, he might be willing to hire you in September if you could go one quarter this summer and finish your degree during subsequent summers as Kast did here. Of course, the salary won't be too good for a non-professional, but it will be enough for you to support your family.

Steen: Gee, I'd appreciate your contacting Lowe. Would it be possible for you to do it this week?

Harper: I'll write him today. As I stated, before though, keep our personal discussions to yourself, especially this proposition.

Later that afternoon, Harper asked Mrs. Snider to accompany him to an empty classroom in the building so that they could discuss a problem he was having. At this time he approached her concerning the Dick Steen incident and she replied that it was probably her fault that Fred was upset. She was the one who had told Pauly. "Apparently I misinterpreted what Dick had said about his conversation with you. Anyway, Dick, look at it from this point of view—I did get Fred to finally do something about our problem of catalog reproduction. I've been after him for a year and this time he finally took some action." To this Harper replied, "I wonder if getting him to implement action is worth placing a strain on personal relationships among three people who must cooperate if the library is going to function properly. I would appreciate your coming to me if there is personal conflict. I don't particularly like being 'called on the carpet' for things that aren't my fault, especially if Fred has to resort to lying."

The conversation ended when Mrs. Snider replied, "I don't think you have to worry. Fred has told me numerous times, 'Dick has the potential of being an outstanding librarian and administrator.' "

On June 1, Pauly called each professional librarian into his office concerning plans for the next year. On May 29, the Board of Regents authorized President Hoyt to offer new contracts to all staff members for the coming year. In this respect, Harper and Pauly held the following conversation:

Pauly: Did you get the raise you were expecting?

Harper: It isn't quite as much as you stated I would get, but it is slightly above that percentage authorized in the governor's 1963-1964 budget. I'm satisfied with it if you're satisfied with my performance this year.

Pauly: We have no complaints. I'm completely satisfied with your progress. I plan to turn over many more duties to you. Now that you have been here a year, I plan for us to really make progress. There are many things I have wanted to do and now feel that you and I will be able to complete some of the really interesting library functions. I find that it takes about one year to find out whether you can trust a subordinate. For instance, when I replace my secretary who is quitting in August, I know that the new person will be miserable for the first year or until I know I can trust her.

Harper: Well, I like to believe I can trust all of my assistants from the beginning. I do hope I have demonstrated that I'm one worthy of trust.

Pauly: I'm sure of it.

Harper: I do have some questions I would like to ask if you have time.

Pauly: Go ahead.

Harper: What action have you taken to get the policies I completed in January approved by the president and the division chairmen as we had originally planned?

Pauly: Well, I decided not to present them to the president until all departments have completed their manuals.

Harper: Aren't their projects procedures, rather than policies, concerning faculty participation in building a working library collection?

Pauly: Yes, but I still think we should wait until he can read everything.

Harper: Well, I was under the impression that you were in a rush to complete them by last January, that's why I'm inquiring now.

Pauly: Do you have other questions?

Harper: Yes. It seems to me that the complete acquisitions procedure breaks down when some materials bypass my department. I'm thinking of things from King Books. We aren't recording near the amount you seem to be purchasing. I also feel that I'm guessing concerning the amount of money left in our budget as a result of your separate purchasing.

Pauly: We can talk about this later.

Harper: Finally, I know Mary plans on working at the library this summer, but have you heard anything from Miss Fish or Mr. Lee concerning the state consultant job?

Pauly: I'm not sure what happened. I didn't understand why Miss Fish told Mary that they didn't have the job in the plans. It surely made me look bad at the time.

Harper: I hope something comes along soon—she is getting impatient. She is looking forward to this summer though.

Pauly: Be sure to have her let your secretary type any materials she needs before she starts teaching. As I told her last week, it would look bad if you did her work while she was teaching.

Harper: Are we still planning on getting the new acquisitions keysort printed? I have been working on it and have it just as I want it. It will be of great benefit in processing orders in the acquisitions and cataloging departments.

THOUGHT QUESTIONS (PART 2)

1. What activities, interactions, and sentiments are required for the successful completion of Mr. Harper's responsibilities?

2. As a result of Mr. Pauly's interview with Mr. Harper, what sources of job satisfaction should Mr. Harper expect?

3. In terms of Mr. Harper's personal job satisfaction, what personal needs remained unsatisfied as of June 1963?

4. In Mr. Harper's case, what is the relationship between job satisfaction and individual development? As a result of Mr. Pauly's emergent behavior, which is most likely to influence Mr. Harper's decision to remain at Eberhard Library?

5. What threat does Mr. Harper's leadership pattern present to Mr. Pauly's leadership status?

6. What information sources did Mr. Pauly use in controlling employee job behavior?

7. Was Mr. Pauly justified in implementing his probation procedure for determining the trustfulness of his secretary and Mr. Harper?

8. What information source is used by Mr. Pauly in becoming aware of the need to formulate a new procedure for catalog card reproduction?

9. Why did Mr. Pauly find it necessary to make a decision on a new catalog card reproduction procedure at the time he did? What possible motives did he have?

10. What steps does Mr. Pauly take in making the decision about changing catalog card reproduction procedures?

PERSONAL CONFLICT

Harper acknowledged his letter of contract, deciding to stay at P.S.C. another year. On June 4, Mrs. Harper began her employment. Her materials were all typed and prepared for duplicating at the campus print shop. Some were returned because of defective stencils. New stencils were being typed by Harper's secretary at the request of Mr. Pauly's secretary.

Two days later, Dick Steen came to Mr. Harper to tell him that he had been offered, and had accepted, a position at Eastern State College. He was very elated with the transactions. He gave all of the credit to Harper who had made the contacts. Steen planned to continue work at Eberhard Library until graduate library school began the 19th of June. After finishing a quarter, he would go to Eastern to work for nine months and then return to graduate library school for further study.

During the next day, Harper and Mrs. Snider spent some time rearranging a form which their departments used for processing materials. No major changes in the form were made; it was a matter of rearranging a number of items in such a way that time could be saved by the student assistants. After completion of the form Harper told Mrs. Snider that he would have it duplicated and implemented immediately. He planned to place one copy in the notebook he was compiling for Mr. Pauly. He would show the changes to Pauly during their next meeting since the form was only concerned with the two departments was was basically the same form he had presented to Fred when it was originally implemented several months ago. Part of Harper's decision not to confer with Pauly immediately was based upon that morning's developments concerning Dick Steen.

Apparently, Dick had mentioned to Mrs. Snider that he was going to work at Eastern. Mrs. Snider mentioned Dick Steen's appointment to Pauly at 10:00. At 10:30, Steen was called to Pauly's office. Pauly told Steen that he did not approve of this transaction. He threatened to call Dr. Short to see if Short would reconsider admitting Steen to graduate library school. Pauly pointed out to Steen that he was the one responsible for Steen's being accepted. Steen's reply to Pauly was, "Do what you please, just so we know where we stand."

After this conversation, Steen told Harper to expect to be "called on the carpet" as he thought Pauly had an idea that Harper was responsible for getting the appointment. Steen was sure, however, that neither Snider nor Pauly knew the actual story.

An hour later, Pauly instructed Mrs. Snider to tell Dick Steen that he was no longer employed at Eberhard Library. His reason was that the policy of the college was to not allow anyone to work on a part-time basis if he were not attending classes. This reason was used by Mrs. Snider, even though she had cleared Steen's employment with Pauly earlier in May.

When Steen told Harper of the coming trouble, Harper told Steen to forget Pauly's threat. Harper told Steen that he knew Dr. Short and that Short wouldn't consider such a request.

At approximately 4:30 that afternoon, Mrs. Snider came to Harper and stated, "Dick, I've done it again. Fred wants you, your wife, Ruby, and any other professionals that can be located in the office at once." She also stated that she had shown Pauly the form that had been completed and Fred "blew his top."

All the librarians went into the office where Pauly ordered Snider to close the door. The discussion began by Pauly stating, "I want everyone to know that I am the one in charge of the library. [pause] A few months ago, Harper told me that Mr. Brown [Brown was not present] resented me because I told the professional librarians that if they didn't like the way I ran the library they could quit. Well, I want to repeat that very statement right now."

The discussion that followed did not emphasize the form which Harper and Snider developed. He mentioned that a statement concerning the color of pencils that were to be used by the different sections was left off. Harper pointed out that he left it off on the first set because he didn't believe it to be of significance anymore as each department was issued a different color. Pauly maintained that it was a matter of personal principle, since he originally had suggested the inclusion of the statement.

Pauly then talked about the fact that Harper's secretary was doing work for Mrs. Harper. He then read a personal memorandum he had written to Mrs. Harper that morning concerning the new stencils. Mrs. Harper had not received the communication prior to the meeting as it was still in her mail box. Mr. Pauly's secretary was called and ordered to go get the memorandum. Mrs. Harper explained why the stencils were being retyped and that she had assumed Pauly knew of the retyping as it was Pauly's secretary who had returned them. This matter was then dropped as a case of poor communication between Pauly and his secretary.

Pauly then proceeded by stating, "I am also making a file of a particular librarian's nasty memos to me." To this, Harper replied, "What memos are you talking about? Do you have an example we can see? If you are accusing one of us, why don't you just say so?" These questions got the following answer, "Well, some people may not consider them nasty, but I'm still making a file of them." (Harper later learned that the memo to which Mr. Pauly was referring was sent by Mr. Brown. Brown had given Mr. Pauly's secretary the note this particular morning—a duplicate copy of a note Mr. Brown had previously sent to Mr. Pauly three months ago.) Today's note was handwritten across the prior message (see Exhibit 6). (Harper received this information from Mr. Pauly's secretary.)

After a long silence, Pauly concluded, "Well, it's five; you are all excused. I think we need things like this to get things off our chests." After the meeting, Pauly made the following comment to Harper while the latter was waiting for his wife to come from her office: "I still think it was wrong for us to send Dick Steen to Eastern."

Harper: Us send?

Pauly: That's what I said. Dick told me you arranged it for him.

EXHIBIT 6

Memorandum to Mr. Pauly

To: FKP   Date 2/23/63

From: Hal Brown, Reference

The RECODAK 501 microfilm reader is out of order. Because all of
our machines have been in great demand, I would appreciate your
contacting the RECODAK repairman at your earliest convenience.
Thank you.

Still out of order 6/7/63

Before leaving on his vacation, Pauly arranged for the Keysort salesman
to meet with Harper concerning the new forms. He also called Harper in to
outline some new projects he had planned. Pauly left for his vacation and did
not return until July 24. Harper finished his annual report while Pauly was
gone and gave it to Pauly on July 24. He read the report and approved it
before Harper left for vacation in August (see **Excerpts from Annual Report,**
p. 72).

While Pauly was on vacation, he closed the main office, had all mail
held until his return, and in a memo to the president he appointed Miss Fels as
the one in charge during his absence. This information was given to the
casewriter by Mr. Pauly's secretary.

EMERGENT BEHAVIOR

In mid-November of 1963, during the usual coffee break at the Memorial
Union, the conversation listed below was taking place among Brown, Kast, and
Harper. Preceding the conversation are highlights of the period from July 30
through December, 1963:

(1)   Since September, Harper had not been requested by Pauly to
attend the regularly scheduled State Library Council meetings. While away
from the office, Pauly placed Miss Fels in charge even though he continually
referred to Harper as the assistant director.

(2)   Mrs. Grace Huxley, Pauly's new secretary, had been told by Pauly
that she was to screen all outgoing mail before sending it to the post office and
that in his absence all incoming mail was to be held until his return. She did,
however, make arrangements with Harper to see that his department's mail was
sent out without delay and she notified Harper of any incoming mail that she
thought might be of value.

(3)   Mrs. Harper had been offered—and accepted—a position at Harris High School as the librarian. Mrs. Harper was responsible for making all of the contacts for securing the position and neither she nor her husband had told Pauly about the position. Pauly was on vacation when the job was offered. He first learned of her employment at Harris High through his son who had been assigned to one of Mrs. Harper's study halls.

On one occasion in early November a graduate student of P.S.C. who was taking library courses in an effort to qualify for a librarian-teacher certificate was informed by the P.S.C. placement office that Harris High had a teacher-librarian opening for January of 1964. Thinking this was Mrs. Harper's present position, she immediately informed Pauly of the listing. Pauly called John Hartshorn, superintendent of schools, concerning the matter. (This conversation, as interpreted by Mr. Hartshorn, is cited below.)

Pauly: John, are the Harpers leaving town in January? If so, I want to know, because I don't want Dick to leave my staff. I'm inquiring because of the listing you gave to the P.S.C. placement office.

John: I don't think you have to worry about their leaving town, but I think you should consult them, not me, concerning their plans. I'm in no position to speak for other people, especially one of my employees. I suggest that next time you contact the parties involved, not me.

The conversation ended at this point. Hartshorn later told Mr. Harper of the incident and that Fred sounded desperate. Hartshorn suggested that Mr. Harper reassure Fred that he was planning to stay at P.S.C. at least for the remainder of the academic year.

(4)   The acquisition keysort form that was ordered in June had not arrived. Harper contacted Pauly about this matter on three separate occasions. Pauly gave the same answer each time. "I don't know what the delay is; I'll call them tomorrow." After the third visit Harper contacted the salesman and found that Pauly had cancelled the order on June 11, 1963, giving no reason for the change in plans. Harper, however, didn't tell Pauly of his contact with the salesman. Instead, he waited two days and reapproached Pauly concerning the materials. Pauly stated that the cards had not arrived and that he had not been able to contact the salesman.

(5)   Pauly continued to issue payment vouchers and orders without telling Harper. These included the two before-mentioned accounts plus orders sent to discount houses for books on pornography and other items of special interest to Pauly. Pauly typed some of these orders at home, had Mrs. Huxley type a few, and on one occasion had Harper's secretary type two vouchers while Harper was out of the office. Harper knew of the proceedings, because of missing voucher numbers and various other process checks he was able to make. He also was informed of the transactions by Mrs. Huxley and his secretary.

These behaviors implemented some of the topics and actions discussed below and it is for this reason that they are included.

Kast: Dick, I was telling Hal that I have a few good offers for library positions. The trouble is, they want someone right now.

Harper: Are you going to take one of these positions?

Kast: You can bet I would like to, but I don't think I will until next year. I want to finish my degree in sociology at P.S.C. before I move to another position. After that I might even get out of the library profession entirely. [Kast received his graduate library degree during the past summer.] Besides, I promised Fred I would stay two additional years.

Harper: I wouldn't let that stop me, especially after you didn't get the raise he promised you upon completion of your library degree.

Kast: That's true, but my record might get a smear if Fred decided to get nasty.

Brown: I also got some notifications from my placement services at Peabody College. I want to thank both of you for writing letters for my file. If the right job comes along and I have enough money saved for moving costs, I'll not be here next year. I told Bette to be prepared to move, just in case I get an acceptable offer.

Harper: I hope you people do get other jobs. I don't want to be the only one who leaves next August. I have even been trying to persuade Ruby to accept one of the two offers she has from Texas and Nebraska. I believe she would leave if she had a little more confidence in her work.

Kast: [Jokingly] Sounds as if you are trying to overthrow the king, Dick.

Harper: Maybe if three or four people decided to leave, the prexy would realize that all is not rosy in the library. Anyway, I don't see how professional librarians can continue to be errand boys for Fred. I know I had planned on being here three years. I bought a home, and except for the dirt and wind have gotten used to the weather, but I couldn't take another year of Pauly. That's why I activated my placement file, applied for graduate study, and scheduled entrance examinations for February.

Brown: I guess it's time to go back.

Harper: It is about that time. Don't forget you two, I need your request lists right away—I'm going to order everything we need. If I don't spend money on your needs and those of the faculty, Pauly will spend it for Henry Miller, sex books, gifts, and such. I already processed your film requests, Jerry. It's going to run us about $5,000 just for essential replacements and urgent requests. Fred is really going to get a shock when he finds out about my ordering so many films.

THOUGHT QUESTIONS (PART 3)

1. How did Mr. Pauly's given sentiments concerning communication flow affect his daily activities in the acquisitions department?

2. In terms of the behavior of the professional librarians, what were the consequences of the communication channels used by Mr. Pauly?

3. How does Mr. Pauly "punish" Mr. Harper and Mr. Brown for their actions as described in the section "Personal Conflict" beginning on page 55?

4. How do you account for the delay in the implementation of the acquisitions keysort card which had been approved by Mr. Pauly?

5. In terms of Mr. Harper's emergent behavior, what is the nature of the information contained in his annual report?

6. What impact did the approved acquisitions policies have upon the effectiveness of Eberhard Library? Upon Mr. Harper's job satisfaction?

A CONFLICT OF VALUES

In late October of 1963, Mr. Harper entered the technical processes area where he found Mr. Pauly browsing through the acquisitions department's "to be ordered" file. The file, which contained processed library requisition cards, was located on Mr. Harper's desk. These cards were to be typed for immediate ordering. Mr. Harper hoped to get the $5,000 order out within the week. He had contemplated sending this order for some time and had previously mentioned it to Pauly. Pauly had agreed that the order was necessary because of the number of back-logged faculty requests.

When Mr. Harper approached, Pauly replaced the file and proceeded to his own office. At the time, neither Pauly nor Harper made mention of the incident. Two days later Harper received a handwritten communication stating, "Dick, do not place any large orders at this time. Continue to send orders in the routine manner as you have previously done."

Harper was upset about this note, but didn't approach Pauly concerning its contents. He continued to send only routine orders and held the large purchase for future consideration.

In late December of 1963, Pauly put the following note on Harper's desk: "$8,000 left in budget." After receiving this note, Harper went to see Pauly. He told Pauly that the $8,000 should be considered as encumbered because the amount of unpaid invoices, materials on order, and standing-order materials that would drift in between now and June would amount to approximately $8,000. Pauly agreed that no more orders should be sent unless there was an emergency request.

Harper sent out no more orders during December and continued in this manner through early January. He did continue to pay invoices for books received and kept close track of the amount expended. On January 14, Pauly asked Mr. Harper to come to his office.

Pauly: The business office notified me just now, stating that we have $2,000 left in the budget. Get me a detailed list of vouchers you have sent out since December 23. I want you to include the voucher number and amount. [Harper found Pauly to be somewhat irritated and nervous.]

Harper: All right, I'll get the figures. I can tell you, though, it won't run over $2,000 since December 23 or even $8,000 since December 1.

Pauly: Well, I thought we had $8,000 when I sent you that note, but I just learned it was closer to $5,000. I need those figures as soon as you can get them.

Harper: Okay. Anything else?

Pauly: No!

Harper then returned to his desk where he began to go through the accounts payable file (see Exhibit 7) to find the number and amount of vouchers issued since December 23. Harper copied each down, but did not include those vouchers issued by Mr. Pauly. Harper's secretary and Pauly's secretary had made a point to list all vouchers issued from Mr. Pauly's office.

EXHIBIT 7

Accounts Payable File (July 1, 1963-June 30, 1964)*

G. Frank

6000	7. 1.63	190.00
6026	7.15.63	125.00
6311	7.24.63	177.75
6743	11.21.63	197.25

A. D. White

6023	7. 2.63	200.00
6024	7.10.63	200.00

King Books

6015	7. 2.63	202.00
6016	7.10.63	212.92
6017	7.18.63	200.39
6018	7.24.63	178.29
6360	9.12.63	196.14
6361	9.15.63	206.55
6603	10.29.63	226.52
6742	11.21.63	206.76
6871	12.13.63	195.67

EXHIBIT 7 (continued)

High Plains Art Center (card 1)

6192	7.27.63	205.00	*2 0 4. 00*
6191	7.29.63	215.00	
6193	7.29.63	24.00	
6194	7.29.63	24.50	
6276	8.15.63	203.00	
6275	8.15.63	100.00	*100.00*
6277	8.16.63	21.75	
6358	9.10.63	201.50	
6359	9.10.63	205.00	
6444	10.10.63	204.00	

High Plains Art Center (card 2)

6445	10.11.63	195.00
6517	11. 8.63	200.00
6518	11. 8.63	204.00
6761	11.27.63	200.00
6762	11.27.63	205.00
6917	12.26.63	204.00
6918	12.27.63	209.00
7104	1.29.64	205.00
7105	1.30.64	215.00

*Selected list of vouchers issued by Mr. Pauly from July 1, 1963 to January 14, 1964. The black-lined items indicate to Mr. Harper that these vouchers have been paid. (See **Excerpts from Acquisitions Manual,** p. 79.)

This was possible because the library was given a block of voucher numbers (see **Excerpts from Acquisitions Manual,** p. 79) by the business office and only one voucher with a given number could be issued by any department on campus. This made it necessary for Mr. Pauly to record or have recorded all voucher numbers he issued. The clerical assistants then made a point to give this information to Harper. He, in turn, would call the business office securing the amount of the voucher, the vendor's name, and a description of the items purchased. This was necessary because Pauly sent the vouchers directly to the business office, keeping all other copies in his desk. When the voucher was paid by the State Treasurer, a white copy was forwarded to Mr. Pauly by the business office. He would then take these out of all vouchers paid, sending the remainder to Harper.

Harper returned to Pauly's office, presenting the information that was requested. The vouchers since December 23 amounted to $1,886.40. He further reported the amount spent since December 1, but Pauly stated that he wasn't interested in the amount spent before December 23.

Pauly then thanked Harper for the information and told Harper to continue to make the vouchers, but to give everything to him after the vouchers were completed. He stated that he would send all vouchers to vendors as he saw fit.

Harper then returned to his desk where he went over the figures concerning vouchers issued by Pauly (see Exhibit 7). It had been apparent to Harper for some time that Pauly had been issuing numerous vouchers each month to A. D. White, King Books, G. Frank, High Plains Fine Arts Center, and other vendors. Harper had made an all-out attempt to keep track of Pauly's vouchers because of two prior incidents.

The first incident occurred on July 1, 1963. This was the first day of the new fiscal year. At this time Harper closed the 1962-63 records. He first went through the "accounts payable file" (see **Excerpts from Acquisitions Manual,** p. 79) to see if all vouchers issued during the period had been paid. He noticed that the only ones that were unpaid were those issued to King Books, G. Frank, and an A. D. White. The vouchers issued to White were the ones that Harper was most concerned about since they all seemed to be for similar amounts (see Exhibit 8). Upon checking other files and the business office, he found that A. D. White resided at 404½ 2d Street in Harris. Being somewhat mystified by these purchases, Harper took the information to Hal Brown.

EXHIBIT 8

Accounts Payable Card (1962-63)

A. D. White		
7071	3.15.63	198.00
7138	4.17.63	195.00

It was Harper's intention to see if Hal knew of this apparent book dealer. When Harper presented the duplicate copy of the voucher to Brown, he did not immediately recognize the book dealer. He did recognize the address as that of Mr. Pauly. Brown then decided that this was Mr. Pauly's mother who presently lived in Pauly's basement.

Harper didn't push the matter further, but returned to his office. He contacted the business office to see if the vouchers listed on the "accounts payable file" card were paid. The business office confirmed the payments, giving the date and check number.

Harper checked other years under the same name and found similar notations. He checked to see if the materials indicated were in the library. He found that some were and others were not. Harper then decided to let the matter ride, but cautioned his secretary to be on the alert for any further vouchers issued to A. D. White.

The second incident occurred in October of 1963. This time the vendor was High Plains Fine Arts Center (see Exhibit 7). The address was that of a local post office box. Harper went to the business office where he asked to see copies of the vouchers and to see if the vouchers were paid. The vouchers had been paid. Harper preferred not to raise suspicion at this time, so instead of asking for copies of invoices and vouchers, he merely copied titles, voucher numbers, and dates of issuance.

Upon checking the titles against the card catalog, he found that many of the items were in the library, but these were books Mr. Pauly had brought back from Chicago where he attended the A.L.A. convention. Mr. Pauly had previously told Harper that the items were paid for by giving a voucher to the Chicago bookseller while in Chicago. Most of the items were rare items ranging in price from $40 to $165 each.

Harper continued to keep track of these items. He checked them against the collection and because of the vagueness of some listings did not locate each item (see Exhibit 9). One invoice listed items that Harper knew were given as gifts to the library by a local high school. Harper was sure of this as the books had arrived while Harper was at work. This was in August 1963. Pauly was not in the library at the time. Harper was supposed to be on vacation, but had gone to the library to finish a Field Study report. Harper could not locate the gift listings that were made by Mr. Pauly's secretary, but called the high school librarian concerning some of the titles. The high school librarian confirmed Harper's suspicion. The high school librarian further stated that the books were a gift to the college library and that no money was involved in the transaction.

Mr. Harper never mentioned his findings to anyone. He did confer with Mr. Brown, seeking information about the High Plains Art Center, but Harper did not disclose his suspicions. Mr. Brown knew of no such book center in Harris, but took the address in an effort to secure some information. Harper's secretary seemed suspicious of the address when she saw it, but made no statements concerning the validity.

Harper contacted Professor Don Black, a lawyer and a personal friend, concerning the conflict-of-interest law. They discussed Harper's liability for signing vouchers without seeing the materials purchased. Harper signed such vouchers when he first began working in the library (see **Excerpts from Acquisitions Manual, p. 79**). At that time Mr. Pauly told Harper to make vouchers for all unpaid invoices that were not processed. Pauly assured Harper at that time that all of the materials were in the library. When Harper met with Black he made no specific mention of the High Plains transactions.

EXHIBIT 9 High Plains Invoice

ORIGINAL ART   RARE BOOKS   PICTURE FRAMING

HIGH PLAINS ART CENTER

Nº 67   P. O. BOX 572
                        HARRIS OKL.   87601

_____19____

TO _____

_____

_____

ITEMS	AMOUNT

FINANCIAL CRISIS

On January 16, 1963, Mr. Pauly asked Harper to make vouchers for twelve pages of items that Pauly had picked from the Metro City Library. The items were bought from the M.C.L. duplicate shelf and were, in Pauly's estimation, of value to P.S. C. students and faculty. After Harper had completed the vouchers, he presented them to Pauly for signatures. Pauly, however, insisted that Harper sign them. Pauly stated that the materials were on the serials processing shelves, and Harper tried in vain to locate the materials.

To be sure that he had no liability concerning this matter, Harper contacted the college lawyer, Don Black. He explained this situation and his suspicions of Pauly's activities. Black was astonished by the latter information, but joined Harper in seriously questioning Pauly's behavior on the basis of the evidence collected. Harper told Black that his greatest fear was that the procedures followed by the library and business office were such that anyone who had access to the records might become suspicious of the activities. Harper disclosed a fear that this information would become circulated to outside sources, or become a basis of investigation by auditors. Harper suggested that such activities would surely lead to an embarrassing situation if the president were to receive the information from sources other than library personnel. Harper told Black that he wasn't contemplating a disclosure to the president unless he could absolutely prove Pauly was violating state laws or until there was a threat that the information was known by other personnel or outside sources.

Harper's main concern was that he suspected his secretary knew something was wrong and that she would begin to formulate her own conclusions. Mr. Harper's secretary had twice been involved in conflicts with Mr. Pauly. The latest concerned Mr. Pauly's deducting one day of her vacation time, because she was forced to stay home with an ill son. She argued that the deduction should have been from her sick leave.

Harper did not know if anyone else was suspicious except Mr. Brown. Black suggested that Harper continue to see Hal concerning the situation thus avoiding a possible showdown where it would be Pauly's word against Harper's. Black advised Harper to continue to collect evidence, but suggested no solution to the situation.

The following day, Hal Brown met with Harper and stated that he had contacted a post office employee concerning the box number listed on the duplicate High Plains invoice. The post office employee reported that the box was "rented to a Mr. Fred Pauly." Brown told Harper that the post office employee didn't know Pauly so no suspicion had been aroused. This information resulted in Harper and Brown keeping in close contact concerning Pauly's activities.

Harper received copies of all High Plains vouchers from the business office and began checking titles of books against the library collection. Brown aided Harper in this investigation. Harper contacted a local printshop concerning the High Plains invoices. He found that the printshop had printed them and received a check from Fred K. Pauly. Although the new developments seemed to point a strong finger of suspicion at Mr. Pauly, Brown and Harper continued to keep the information to themselves. They felt that many of the activities were suspicious, but the nature of recording acquisitions in the library prior to 1962 limited concrete proof.

On March 8, 1964, as Mr. Harper was leaving his office for lunch, Mrs. Huxley showed a voucher she had just typed for Mr. Pauly. It was made out to the High Plains Fine Art Center in the amount of $205. Mrs. Huxley mentioned this matter to Harper because Mr. Pauly had allowed her to send to vendors approximately twenty previously completed vouchers. These had been completed by Mr. Harper's personnel. Mrs. Huxley stated that she was to take them to the business office with the one for High Plains. Harper then asked if all of the others that he had initiated had been processed. Mrs. Huxley stated that there were some twenty-five still in Pauly's office. She pointed to the High Plains voucher and asked Harper if he knew who owned the bookshop.

Harper: Why do you ask?

Huxley: Because I think someone is padding his pocket.

Harper: What makes you think so?

Huxley: I've suspected it ever since I began typing High Plains vouchers. First, I noticed that Mr. Pauly trusted no one. That in itself raised my suspicions. When he told me not to let you or your secretary have the extra copy of these vouchers, I knew something was wrong. To confirm my suspicion, I recognized some of the titles as being on a gift list I typed last September. In fact, I have decided to make myself a file of these voucher copies just in case something goes wrong. I don't want to be caught in any suspicious activities.

Harper: Does anyone else suspect anything?

Huxley: Not that I know of. [pause] Mr. Pauly rents post office box 595, doesn't he?

Harper: I suspect he does, but I prefer we not tell anybody of our suspicions.

Huxley: To think that my income tax money goes toward Mr. Pauly's home. Things like this make me mad. Income taxes are bad enough without having to put money in other people's pockets.

Harper: There isn't anything we can do about this situation except to continue keeping ourselves informed and keeping files of vouchers as you have been doing. I wouldn't leave the file in your desk at night. It wouldn't be the first time something disappeared from a locked desk.

Huxley: Oh, I know; Mr. Pauly has a key to every desk in the building. Another thing I'm puzzled about is the fact that Mr. King has been calling about every other day concerning some unpaid invoices. Each time he calls, Mr. Pauly issues one or two vouchers.

Since January, however, Mr. Pauly hasn't sent but one or two a month. Lately, Mr. Pauly has told me to tell Mr. King that he is in conference and can't be bothered. Do you think they're in this together?

Harper: I never thought there was a connection.

Huxley: Have you considered asking Mr. Pauly about any of this? That's what Dear Abby suggests in such situations.

Harper: I have tried twice to suggest that conflict of interest is prohibited by state law. Once I brought up the subject of the recent Kansas State Fair scandal where an agent of the state had purchased supplies for the fairgrounds from a family-owned company. The official was later forced to resign. I also picked an opportune time to discuss the recent New Jersey library scandal. This involved a director of libraries who was arrested for selling library materials and was involved in other illegal activities. Mr. Pauly seemed indifferent to the two subjects except that in the latter case a $42 *Exotica 3* was on my desk the same afternoon. *Exotica 3* had been missing since December of 1963. I'm not sure whether my mentioning the New Jersey case, or my comments written on the in-process keysort did the trick. [The following comment was written on the keysort: "Arrived 11.24.63, taken home by Mr. Pauly 11.24.63 without being processed, stamped with ownership stamp, or checked out.]

Huxley: I doubt if you could approach him any other way. He's the boss and no one is going to tell him anything! I doubt if anyone would believe you anyway. He has such a way with people that he could convince even the president that these activities are justified.

On March 24, 1963, Mr. Brown approached Mr. Harper about a possible solution to the dilemma. Brown, who now knew of Mrs. Huxley's suspicions, suggested that Dr. Bob Howser, assistant to the president and close friend of Brown, be informed of the situation. Brown thought that this was the time to at least hear suggestions from an administrator. Brown and Harper had found that the further their investigation was carried, the more critical the situation appeared. For instance, Brown had contacted two or three students who had given him personal checks to cover microfilm charges, lost reference books, reference book fines, and photocopy charges. In every case involving sums above $3 the check had been cashed at the Memorial Union. After Mr. Brown received the checks or cash he gave them to Mr. Pauly. As Mr. Brown did not issue receipts for these transactions, the amount of money was never subject to the college audit. Brown, however, kept a close record of the amount of money turned in to Mr. Pauly. This amounted to about $200 per year. This was not the procedure for money collected at the circulation desk. Official receipts were given for all transactions and the money was taken by Mr. Kast to the business office. Mrs. Huxley reported that she had taken only $15 or $20 to the business office during the current academic year. Mr. Brown reported that he alone had turned in $110 during the same period. Mrs. Huxley also had reported receiving $15 or $20 from students who owed fines from previous quarters. She stated that she knew that certain students were paying fines directly to Mr. Pauly. This was the procedure that was recently started whereby students could not register for a new quarter without first paying unpaid library fines.

Brown stated that he had begun to stay awake nights worrying about the situation and wanted to know if Harper had given further consideration to a solution. Brown thought one alternative would be to see Bob Howser the following week. This would be about three weeks before the president returned from his six-month trip to Panama as a representative of the State Department.

After a discussion of this plan and other alternatives, Harper gave approval to Brown's suggestion. It was agreed that Brown would call Howser on Wednesday evening and ask him to go for a ride where he would introduce the problem. Brown would then bring Howser to the library where Harper could go into detail on the situation. Wednesday night was Harper's night to be on duty. Mr. Pauly also was out of town on library business.

REQUIRED BEHAVIOR

Even though the above situations were the focus of Harper's and Brown's attention, they performed their regular duties as if the problems had not existed. Harper continued to perform his teaching duties, oversee the acquisitions department, work with faculty on planning new purchases to strengthen subject areas, and spend two to four hours daily working with Dr. Cross of the Department of Education as part of the campus-wide Improvement of Instruction Committee project. The committee was one on which Mr. Pauly served. Pauly was responsible for Harper's being invited to participate in the project. The project was an attempt to combine library education with classroom instruction. Harper assisted Dr. Cross in elementray education. He presented library materials, designed laboratory projects, developed bibliographies, and participated in class discussions. When Harper was asked to handle the project, Pauly stated that Harper was the only librarian with an interest in this area.

The success of Harper's program stemmed from the cooperation he received from other library staff members. Miss Fels, Mrs. Kast, Miss Noblot, and Mr. Brown assisted Harper in the project with enthusiasm. Harper conferred with Pauly about the project at frequent intervals. Pauly stated that it appeared to be a success and that Harper should prepare a written report for study by the Improvement of Instruction Committee.

Pauly had asked Harper to accompany him on two trips in March. Harper declined both times. Pauly also asked Harper to make a trip to Norman, Oklahoma to take part in a two-day orientation of IBM instruction in relation to the Union List of Serials' project. Harper did not attend this activity because his wife had recently returned from the hospital. None of the other librarians were approached concerning these trips.

Mr. Pauly was out of town attending various conferences and library building planning projects during this period. He sent word to the president to the effect that Harper was in charge while he was gone. On two occasions, Pauly specifically called Harper into his office to show him the reports which indicated Harper was in charge. Harper was not in charge during the period of June 1963 through February 1964.

It was also during this period that Mr. Pauly conferred with all professional librarians concerning their plans for the coming year. These inquiries were requested by the president's secretary so that the president could budget for salaries and positions for the next academic year. Although the recommendations were due in February, the president did not send letters of appointment until May 20, 1964, at which time the Board of Regents met to consider faculty appointments for the coming year.

Harper told Pauly that at the present time he was planning to return for the 1964-65 academic year. Harper did point out that the final decision rested upon the amount of salary increase and library situation at that time. Pauly accepted this answer without question.

Mr. Kast and Mr. Brown also told Pauly that they planned to return. Both men, however, told Harper that they were seeking new positions.

THOUGHT QUESTIONS (PART 4)*

1. How effective is the overall purchasing process as developed by the Prairie State College business office?

2. Can Mr. Harper justify his actions concerning purchases made by Mr. Pauly?

3. What are some of the possible reasons that Mr. Black might suggest Mr. Harper seek Mr. Brown's assistance in investigating local booksellers?

4. What advice would you give Mr. Harper after his investigation of various purchase orders initiated by Mr. Pauly?

5. Can Mr. Brown justify his role in the investigations?

6. What is your reaction to the memo concerning misuse of authority with regard to budget and mails (Exhibit 4, dated April 8, 1964, page 39).

7. How much control does the business office have in terms of library expenditures? How much control does Mr. Pauly have? How much control do library users have?

8. What effects could Mr. Pauly's purchases have upon collection development at Eberhard Library?

*More Thought Questions follow the various Excerpts in the proceeding sections.

EXCERPTS

**Annual Report of the Acquisitions Librarian of Eberhard
Library on the Operations and Conditions of the
Acquisitions Department
Fiscal Year 1 July 1962 - 30 June 1965**

INTRODUCTION

In September, 1962, one new professional member was added to the
library staff of Eberhard Library. With this addition to the staff the acquisitions department was reorganized as a separate department of the Library.
From September, 1955, to September, 1962, the director of the library had
functioned as the acquisitions librarian. The acquisitional functions were in
turn performed by members of the office staff.

The functions of the new acquisitions department and acquisitions
librarian stem from the acquisitional policy of the library which is prescribed
in *Acquisitions Organization, Policies, and Procedures Manual of the Eberhard
Library.* Under the direction of the acquisitions librarian the department is
responsible for (1) assisting in book selection, (2) coordinating acquisition
activities for all desired materials, except for those handled directly by the
documents department, whether by purchase, gift or exchange, (3) initiating
and keeping acquisitions records, (4) preparing materials for the catalog
and serials department, and (5) serving as a clearing house for information
regarding publications, publishers, dealers, prices, and book markets. Except
for the purchasing of supplies, equipment, miscellaneous book materials, and
accounts with King Books (5th and Oak, Harris) and G. Frank (1234 Broadway,
Baltimore, Maryland) which are handled through the Office of the Director, the
work of the acquisitions department included the bibliographic verification
of all requests for book orders, the preparation of purchase orders, the
maintenance of records, and communications with faculty and staff concerning
acquisitions of library materials.

Upon approval of the director, the acquisitions department—during my
first year as acquisitions librarian—was highlighted by:

1. Improved communication between faculty and the acquisitions department
   promoted by the issuance of the acquisitions policies of Eberhard
   Library written by Richard Harper and approved by Fred K. Pauly,
   Director.

2. The approval of Fred K. Pauly of the completed *Acquisitions
   Organization, Policies, and Procedures Manual* prepared by Richard
   Harper.

3. The installation of a new verification system resulting in the almost
   complete elimination of purchasing by mistake unneeded duplicate
   copies of materials that were requested as first copies for the library
   collection.

4. The installation of a one-file on-order card system resulting in the
   consolidation of five files under the older system, the simplification

in locating the source of all incoming materials except gifts and exchanges, ease of processing and distribution of materials by listing distribution on the on-order cards, and a fifty per cent reduction of processing time.

5. The establishment of a faculty notification system for processed items resulting in many gratifying responses from faculty and staff and bringing about closer communication between the library and college.

6. The near completion of an over-all program to simplify renewal and handling procedures of subscriptions by transferring as far as possible all direct periodical purchasing to purchasing through subscription jobbers (429 transferred from October 1962 - June 1963) and establishing common expiration dates for all subscriptions.

7. The completion of a keysort coding system for acquisition keysort records, facilitating the securement of information form these records for purchasing, faculty request, budgetary, and other miscellaneous purposes.

8. The introduction of a new letter order from and a new in-process work form which have reduced—and the planning of a new faculty notification-acquisitions keysort card which will reduce—the amount of typing required for placing orders, processing materials, and notifying faculty and staff concerning new acquisitions.

9. Initiation of a program to standardize mailing addresses for all purchased materials and for gift materials when card inquiries for change of address were received, thus eliminating needless delay in distribution of incoming materials.

10. Initiation of an in-process keysort system that enables the acquisitions department to locate requested materials during the processing period or before the book is listed in the card catalog. (This was very beneficial during the period in which the catalog department had a large backlog of materials processed but not listed in the card catalog.)

SERVICE TO USERS

The year has been marked by many gratifying responses by faculty concerning the notification as to the availability of specific materials that have been requested. The notification has been made at the time the processing of the material is completed. This has eliminated faculty calls to the director and acquisitions librarian concerning requests of badly needed materials.

In many instances faculty members have given immediate attention to the faculty notification by calling for the material upon hearing of its availability. The notices have been of particular value in times where delay in filing catalog cards in the main catalog has been apparent. It is felt that the notification to faculty of availability of materials they have requested has increased the communication between the college and the library. Planning has already been done concerning improvement of the present system of notification. An order of a newly designed and greatly improved acquisitions keysort card is to be placed in the near future.

The acquisitions department has sent various correspondence concerning materials information that is thought to be of value or which will result in the avoiding of needless repetition in passing on information. Examples of this are the notification of new standing orders placed for large blocks of materials or notifications concerning the acquisitions of complete listing of materials. The faculty has also been notified concerning book exhibits, results of bibliographic checks of important bibliographies, and other miscellaneous information that may be of interest, or has been requested.

In addition to the faculty notifications and regular services to patrons, the acquisition librarian initiated projects that strive for better library service in general. These projects may be done within the department or by students, when available, taking "Problems in Library Science."

During the past year two such projects were completed. After editing and updating, the projects will be made available to departments of the college, interested individuals, high schools, and other libraries desiring such compilations. One project, "A Subject and Grade Level Index to Home Economics Curriculum Guides in Eberhard Library," is expected to expedite library service to students of PSC who must work with such materials in their studies at the college and present a listing of the holdings of these guides to home economics teachers, curriculum directors, or others throughout the area who may find them of value. The index will the the only guide to the holdings of the library as these are in most cases uncataloged materials found only through indexes located in the documents department.

The other project is of value to elementary teachers of reading. It is concerned with the availability of Newbery and Caldecott books in local libraries. Future projects are planned and plans for distribution and printing have been discussed with the director.

ACQUISITIONS LIBRARIAN ACTIVITIES

As expressed in the personal interview between the director and the acquisitions librarian and prior to the time of hiring, the acquisitions librarian was to act as assistant director of the library directly responsible to the director. In accordance with Section I, Chapter II, pages five to seven of *Acquisitions Organization, Policies, and Procedures Manual of the Eberhard Library* as approved by the director in January, 1963, the acquisitions librarian has been responsible for several undertakings. Projects now in progress include the writing of a *Binding Procedures and Policy Manual;* the collection and study of various forms used in Eberhard Library; the reorganizing and establishment of vertical files for the Western collection, local history collection, and college departmental file which will include reading lists, courses of study, and outlines; and the writing of details for the new special collections librarian, a position which may be filled by September of 1964.

Projects finished or under guidance—in addition to those initiated as acquisitions librarian—include the compiling of information to be used by the director in connection with the proposed new library building; the

supervision of the library at Memorial Hospital; the compiling of information
to be presented to the director for use in the NCATE committee visitation;
the supervising of the microfilming activities in the library; and other miscellaneous
activities.

The acquisitions librarian also was in charge of Books on Exhibit which
was housed in the library for six weeks. He visited various PSC classes to
discuss library services and functions, guided tour of visiting high school
honor students through the library, and supervised displays in the lobby
during the regular sessions.

Mr. Harper also served on the Executive Council of the State Library
Association as publicity director for the organization, participated in the
activities of the State Department of Education, School Library Services
concerning school libraries in the state, helped in making local arrangements
for the Region I Conference of the State Library Association held on the
PSC campus, was active in all State Library Association activities, worked with
Dr. Gordon Orb concerning activities of the Educational Field Service of
PSC, and was active in a program concerning educational programs in
undergraduate colleges offering library science courses which was discussed
at the Library Association conference held in Tulsa. Mr. Harper also
attended and participated in the activities of the State Library Council.

During the year the acquisitions librarian also taught one library
science course and supervised two students in individual projects that were
taken for credit. Mention of these was given earlier.

Acquisitions Organization, Policies and Procedures Manual
Eberhard Library, Prairie State College

INTRODUCTION

Organization of the Eberhard Library. The eight departments of the
Eberhard Library were organized primarily on the basis of the form of
materials handled (serials, documents, special collections) and by the functions
performed by the library (acquisitions, cataloging, reference, circulation, and
bibliography). Each department is indirectly responsible to the director of
the library through the assistant director who has been delegated certain
responsibilities. Specific duties of the assistant director are discussed in
Chapter II, Section 1.

SECTION 1

II. The Acquisitions Department. The acquisitions department of the
Eberhard Library is under the responsibility of the acquisitions librarian
who will also function as the assistant director of the library. The functions
of the acquisitions department stem from the acquisitional policy of the
library (see Section 2, ACQUISITION POLICIES OF THE EBERHARD
LIBRARY).

This department is responsible for: (1) assisting in book selection, (2)
coordinating acquisition activities for all desired materials whether by

purchase, gift, or exchange, (3) initiating and keeping acquisition records, (4) preparing materials for the catalog and serials department where further processing will be done, (5) serving as a clearing house for information regarding publications, publishers, dealers, prices, and book markets.

Organization. The functions of the acquisitions department bring about certain tasks which may be done by professional librarians or non-professional library assistants. Although precise functions are devised for each member of the acquisitions staff, circumstances may arise whose nature causes a deviation from such outlined processes and, in turn, prompt changes as to who is to perform the task. Outlined below are the functions of each member of the acquisitions department.

Assistant Director of the Library. The assistant director is appointed by the director and is directly responsible to the director. The primary objective of the position is to aid and assist the director of the library in the following:

1. Provide leadership for all academic affairs of the library.
2. Represent the director at meetings when it is not possible for the director to attend.
3. Speak before various groups where a representative of the library is needed and the director is not available.
4. Initiate programs or activities in areas dealing with the library where it is felt that there is a particular need.
5. Conduct special research that is of general interest to the library.
6. Coordinate activities of the library.
7. Carry out special assignments.

Acquisitions Librarian. The acquisitions librarian is concerned with the development of plans and policies and their implementation, as well as with the direction and supervision of operations. More specifically, the acquisitions librarian will be responsible for the following:

1. Preparation of the yearly acquisitions budget estimate.
2. Materials selection.
3. Interviewing booksellers' and publishers' representatives, and visiting book stores.
4. Dividing requests and work materials for checking and bibliographic searching.
5. Separating requests for materials as to the type of handling; URGENT, priority, or hold [see Section 3, page 52 in the manual].
6. Assigning of selected bibliographies and book lists for checking.
7. Verification of more difficult entries.
8. Separating all verified entries into those for purchase and those to be requested as gifts and exchanges.

9. Separating materials for purchase according to sources to be used in purchase (jobber, publisher, central agent, etc.).

10. Sorting unfilled requests for unavailable materials into files which will make it convenient when checking dealers' catalogs and lists for needed material.

11. Signing letter and purchase orders.

12. Notifying the serials department of new subscriptions that have been placed.

13. Preparing letters in regard to orders, reports, and policies.

14. Accepting of gift material and distributing it for gift and exchange handling.

15. Making arrangements for transportation of gifts that have been accepted by the director or acquisitions librarian.

16. Forwarding information to typist in regard to sending letters of acknowledgement to donors of gifts accepted by the library.

17. Separating incoming materials according to type of order that will be used.

18. Giving assistance in correcting errors in shipments.

19. Preparing letters in regard to errors discovered in shipments.

20. Checking letter orders and invoices for overdue materials which should be claimed.

21. Preparing letters in regard to claims.

22. Approving invoices after preliminary approval by those doing checking.

23. Sorting and checking invoices for payment.

24. Approving monthly statements.

25. Deciding on and assigning material to various collections in the library.

26. Decisions concerning rare book, pamphlet, gift, and exchange material.

27. Notifying catalog department of special handling and characteristics of certain materials.

28. Checking to see that material has been distributed correctly.

29. Sorting work sheets for notification of departments, faculty, and staff.

30. Checking and distributing acquisition records for filing.

31. Consulting with business office personnel to learn if acquisition department procedures are in keeping with those of the business office.

SECTION III

III. Preparation of Purchase Orders. Payment for library materials is handled on two different forms. Except for the placing of subscription orders, making advanced deposits (UNESCO publications, Library of Congress Card Division, etc.), and forwarding advance payment for materials that can only be purchased in this manner, all library materials *must be* in the library before payment can be made. Payment can NOT be made, except in the above-mentioned cases, until an invoice is received and attached for payment.

Payment by Use of the Voucher. [see sample, page 76 of the manual] The voucher or purchase order is issued when materials and invoices are received. To complete the voucher, the clerical assistant will have received from the acquisitions librarian the keysort card and the duplicate copy of the letter order which have been marked accordingly. In cases where a book is on the invoice, but was not received, the cost of the book is deleted from the purchase order. If a book is back ordered, the keysort is returned to the on-order file, but the duplicate copy of the letter order will be filed just as if all materials were received and a purchase order is forwarded. This is possible because the letter order information is on the keysort making it easily identifiable. It is necessary, however, to make the letter order with a "B.O." to indicate that the book was back ordered. If the invoice indicates that the materials requested are out of print, the keysort is filed in the out-of-print file and the letter order marked "O.P."

The Format of the Voucher. The voucher as well as the agency purchase order [see sample, page 79 of the manual] serves the purpose of: (1) informing the vendor of receipt of the material by the library, (2) notifying the business office concerning payment, (3) notifying the state purchasing agent for issuing payment to the vendor, (4) and establishing a record of payment for the library, vendor, etc.

1. Copies of the voucher
    a. White confirmation copy (attach the "Attention, Vendor!" slip)
    b. Green (Fund) Prairie State College business office accounting copy
    c. Pink agency remittance copy
    d. Duplicate white departmental copy (Returned to library after payment, it is then stamped with date and ownership stamp and filed in the paid voucher books)
    e. Carbon copy (A carbon copy is also made for departmental use only and if filed in unpaid purchase order file until paid, and then put in paid purchase order file)
2. General information typed on voucher
    a. Initials of the typist
    b. Fund number (Changed quarterly by the business office where it originates)
    c. Identification (Always 3)
    d. Agency identification (Always 246)
    e. Account number (02 or 99 depending on the business office who contacts the library requesting a change from one number to the other)
    f. Enc. Doc. No. (Assigned by business office and changed quarterly)

g. Voucher number (Filled in by business office when payment is made)

h. Purchase order number (*Chronological order in number blocks assigned by the PSC business office*)

Disposition of the Voucher. After the voucher is typed and signed by the acquisitions librarian, the vendor's confirmation copy is mailed to the vendor. The remaining copies are given to the clerical assistant who types the date, purchase order, and amount on the vendor's care in the "accounts payable" file [see sample, page 78 of the manual]. She also totals all voucher payment for each day to keep a running total of expenditures which is kept for each fiscal year.

All remaining copies plus the original invoice are then forwarded to the business office. The duplicate letter order and duplicate invoices are then forwarded to the filing assistant who placed them in the processed order file. The keysort card which has had the date and number of the purchase order typed in the right-hand corner under the letter order information is also filed [see sample, page 72 of the manual]. It is placed in the keysort file which is arranged alphabetically by main entry.

Accounts Payable File Card

UNIVERSITY of Kansas Press			
6836	1.18.63	12.50	
6693	11. 7.62	5.00 subs.*	5.00

*Black-lined items indicate that the voucher has been paid. The figure that follows the item indicates the actual amount paid.

THOUGHT QUESTIONS (SUMMARY)

1. What specific environmental factors and required behavior had the greatest impact upon the job satisfaction of Mr. Pauly? Mr. Harper? Mr. Brown? Mr. Kast? Mrs. Snider?

2. Which of Mr. Pauly's leadership skills had the most influence upon the behavior of professional and clerical staff.

3. What effect did Mr. Pauly's behavior have upon clerical employees? Book selection?

4. How does one account for Mr. Pauly's professional success in state library activities as compared to his leadership role at Eberhard Library?

5. How were Mr. Pauly's professional skills related to his job behavior?

6. How important were Mr. Pauly's human-relations skills with regard to the decision-making processes of the Library?

7. How does Mr. Harper's job descriptions compare with his emergent behavior? What are some of the possible reasons for any differences?

8. How would you account for the fact that "as of July 1964" neither Mr. Brown nor Mr. Kast had initiated the final steps in securing other positions?

9. How are professional training and emergent activities integrated in the case?

10. What part does information flow play in the coordination of PSC operations?

11. How does the personnel system at Eberhard Library relate to BBPS?

FOOTNOTES

[1] Prairie State College, "A Self-Study Report" (Harris, U. S.A.: PSC, July 1, 1962).

[2] Henry Miles was director from 1941 to 1954. He was a noted western historian. He did not receive a graduate library degree.

BASIC REFERENCES

Homans, George C. *The Human Group* (New York: Harcourt, Brace, 1950). For examples of case analysis see Chapters 3, 7, 13, and 14.

Zaleznik, Abraham and David Moment. *Dynamics of Interpersonal Behavior* (New York: Wiley, 1964). Contains sample analyses in most chapters.

CHAPTER VI

EFFECTIVE PERSONNEL MANAGEMENT:
TODAY AND TOMORROW

One BBPS requirement not yet fully considered is its functional relationship to strategic long-range planning. Strategic planning efforts provide direction and focus for future growth of library resources and services. This is achieved through a process of deciding on long-range goals, policies, and strategies that are to govern the acquisition, use, and development of library resources.[1]

The identification of necessary cause and effect environmental factors, as depicted in Figure 1A (a duplication of Figure 1, page 20), is a function of the strategic planning process. Strategic plans are implemented through operational planning processes. The behavioral requirements depicted in the conceptualizaton of BBPS are a result of such planning. Operational personnel planning consists of detailed, uniform, and comparatively complete sets of personnel requirements associated with the ongoing administration of the library, e.g., position descriptions, job specifications, performance standards, work rules, and so forth. Operational personnel planning attempts through behavioral requirements to assure that human resources are obtained and used effectively and efficiently in the accomplishment of strategic library goals.

Dynamic operational planning assumes that strategic planning is to be implemented for some set of behavioral requirements (required activities, required interactions, required sentiments, given sentiments and values) that are already taking place in an ongoing organization. Since required and given behavior already exist, strategic planning should involve changes in library goals and objectives as a result of analyzing emergent behavior in terms of collected empirical data. Thus, documented emergent behavior may serve as a starting point for strategic planning efforts. The data collected by monitoring the emergent behavior must become available for use in future decision-making. The broker line connecting required behavior, emergent behavior, organizational image and environmental factors, as depicted in Figure 1A, is shown to emphasize the continuity between emergent behavior and organizational change. Such continuity is the aim of BBPS. One must realize that the actual changes that can be made from day-to-day are limited and that changes can only come about through the long-range strategic planning process.

THE FUNCTION OF MANAGERIAL INFORMATION

Monitoring the interplay between required behavior and emergent behavior, in most cases, is less specific and less reliable than information on

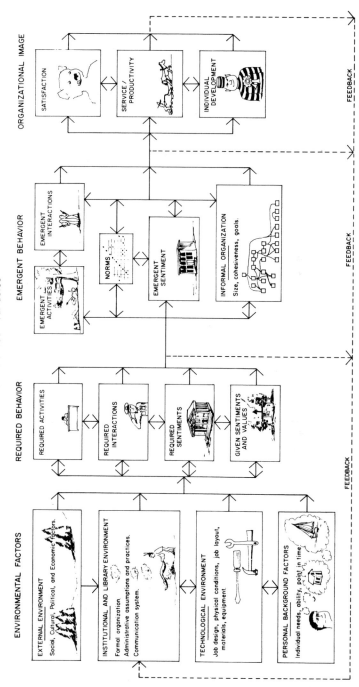

Figure 1A

BEHAVIORAL-BASED PERSONNEL SYSTEM
Relations Between Variables

required behavior. Moreover, the absence of an adequate behavioral frame of reference allows one to ignore the existence or a discrepancy between emergent and required behavior or otherwise fail to accomplish a behavioral change. Both kinds of information are needed. For behavior exhibited today, it is critical that a perspective on behavioral-based personnel systems is developed. At the same time, information on emergent behavior is meaningful only if it can be regarded as making an incremental contribution to some explicitly stated long-range desired goal.

Behavioral-based personnel data will provide a tentative explanation for certain cause-and-effect relationships between what is required and what emerges. Such an approach becomes the basis for a systematic inquiry into any aspect of the broad question of how the recruitment, selection, and utilization of human resources by and within the library might be made more effective.

INFORMATION GATHERING

The operation of BBPS requires library administrators to explore three informational questions: (1) what is? (2) what is desired? and (3) what is to be changed? Determining what is and what is desired involves administrative personnel in collecting information about each variable depicted in Figure 1A. Determining what is to be changed involves administrative personnel in using collected information to reduce discrepancies between required and emergent behavior.

Library planners must be precise about the kinds of personnel data collected. BBPS identifies: (1) the actual inputs (costs of providing personnel, facilities, supplies, and materials) through an analysis of environmental factors, (2) the desired and actual behavioral requirements (activities, inter-actions, sentiments, values, and norms) through an analysis of behavioral patterns, and (3) the desired and actual outputs (observable and measurable changes in service and behavior of library personnel) through an analysis of the organizational image.

Once the library administrator or his advisory staff knows with reasonable certainty the actual and desired state of library resources, processes, and organizational image and has a way of monitoring future states of the system in behavioral terms, he is in a position to assess the effectiveness and efficiency of any operational aspect of the library.

Consequently, it is important that the library administrator not only understand personnel techniques and procedures, but also the techniques for continually updating personnel data. Such data gathering provides alternative solutions to behavioral-based personnel problems.

To a great extent the library administrator should be a competent student of research. He must be able to interpret and plan research programs for use in the organization. The library administrator must be someone who analyzes problems systematically and seeks solutions creatively.

In terms of the behavioral model presented in this book several types of research are applicable. Local research efforts can be as sophisticated or simple as the situation warrants. Experimental research techniques may provide information useful in analyzing the organizational image as a result of varying administrative practices or other background factors. Such information would have aided Mr. Pauly in assessing the behavior of civil service employees at Prairie State as a result of his choice of leadership behavior.

Documented in depth observation of actual situations is an effective data gathering tool which can provide evidence of problem situations. Such case studies involve observation, reporting, interviewing, listening, and discrimination of relevant data. BBPS provides a structure for such data gathering. Chapter V of this book presents data that explains the cause-and-effect relationship between worker dissatisfaction and autocratic leadership.

The literature analysis research technique can be beneficial in confirming or refuting hypotheses about human behavior. An analysis of organizational based data in terms of behavioral research findings could result in decisions that have a positive effect on personnel, especially where such decisions are a result of newly acquired skills for dealing with people.

The attitude survey provides effective organizational data in regard to sentiments and morale level of personnel. Attitude surveys can measure the effects of any number of organizational variables including supervision, promotional opportunities, physical facilities, salaries, and so forth.

French's discussion on personnel department research activities also directs attention to two other less complex levels of research data which might be of value to library administrators—between-library surveys and statistical analysis.[2] Between-library surveys can provide data from other libraries on salaries and so forth in an effort to show the typical practice with respect to employee requirements. The analysis and collection of statistical data can provide information on such matters as turnover, absenteeism, and the like. Statistical data analysis is often overlooked as a source for becoming aware of the need to change or as a source for justifying case studies, experimental research, or attitude surveys.

It is through carefully structured information data banks that library administrators analyze and evaluate required and emergent behavior. Providing the proper balance between what is required and what emerges necessitates a constant recycling of managerial information which identifies discrepancies and alternative courses of action.

SUMMARY

This book began with a relatively simple model of personnel administration and developed from it a simple approach to people as people in library organizations. A conceptualization of the variables which are necessary in analyzing and predicting the behavior of members of work groups was then introduced. This model was a behavioral-oriented systems approach to operational decision-making. A basic model of skill-level competencies was developed to aid in the identification of necessary skill development. Finally, by relating BBPS as an operational planning model to strategic long-range planning processes and by suggesting how research techniques may help accomplish an understanding of the cause-and-effect relationship between actual and required behavior a framework for personnel administration was accomplished. Such a frame of reference should be helpful to library administrators who are attempting to develop effective and efficient operational systems in their local library or library district.

BBPS is a pragmatic approach to viewing managerial functions. Its implementation will depend upon the recognition that:

1. Tasks, people, and organizations are distinct problems.
2. Different skills are appropriate for handling each of these problems.
3. Different skill-mix patterns are implied for different levels, by different people, at different times.
4. The education of library administrators must be interdisciplinary rather than "professional," technical, or task oriented.

The one enduring objective is the effort to develop library administrators who constantly readjust their behavior to the ever-changing environment about them. Leonard Sayles has put is most succinctly:

> Many managers assume positions of executive responsibility with a topsy-turvy view of their world. They have been taught that, in a 'good' organization, a manager spends his time making key decisions, planning, and 'motivating' subordinates. When they find their jobs quite different from the ideal, they are likely to blame the petty frictional elements and bide their time, waiting for the kind of job that will have the anticipated heroic proportions.
>
> But the essence of management is not of heroic proportions. Rather, most managerial behavior is mundane—and frustrating. As we have seen, it involves endless negotiations, trades, and bargaining; meticulous assessment of the state of the organization system; and redirection of one's own and one's subordinates' activities in the light of the information derived from monitoring.
>
> This is the normal state of affairs, not the abnormal or unusual. The price of specialization, multiple experts, and hierarchies is the unworkability of traditional management theories and practices with their neat equating of authority and responsibility and unitary direction. But because organizational behavior is not predicted nor mirrored by the organization chart, one need not despair. The challenge of fulfilling these positions is not a modest one. Enormous personality energy is required to interact in as diverse and multiple roles as those encompassed by the typical executive position.[3]

Effective personnel administration requires people who can deal with behavioral battles that are never won, but only fought well. The success of any library administrator will be measured in terms of his ability to maintain a system of library service which reflects library users—other people.

FOOTNOTES

[1] For a brief discussion of planning levels, see Robert E. Kemper, "Library Planning: The Challenge of Change," in *Advances in Librarianship,* edited by Melvin Voight, Vol. 1 (New York: Academic Press, 1970), pp. 215-18.

[2] Wendell French, *The Personnel Management Process,* 2d. ed. (Boston: Houghton-Mifflin Company, 1970), pp. 519-80.

[3] Leonard Sayles, *Managerial Behavior* (New York: McGraw-Hill, 1964), pp. 259-60.

READINGS FOR FUTURE EXPLORATION

Applewhite, Philip B. *Organizational Behavior* (Englewood Cliffs, N.J.: Prentice-Hall, Inc., 1965).

Argyris, Chris. *Integrating the Individual and the Organization* (New York: John Wiley & Sons, Inc., 1964).

Atkinson, John. *A Theory of Achievement Motivation* (New York: John Wiley & Sons, Inc., 1966).

Bass, Bernard M. *Organizational Psychology* (Boston: Allyn and Bacon, Inc., 1965).

Beer, Michael. *Leadership, Employee Needs, and Motivation* (Columbus, Ohio: The Ohio State University, 1966).

Bell, Gerald D. (ed.). *Organizations and Human Behavior* (Englewood Cliffs, N.J.: Prentice-Hall, Inc., 1967).

Bennis, Warren G. *Changing Organizations* (New York: McGraw-Hill Book Company, 1966).

Berelson, Bernard, and Gary A. Steiner. *Human Behavior: An Inventory of Scientific Findings* (New York: Harcourt, Brace & World, Inc., 1964).

Carzo, Rocco, Jr., and John Yanouzas. *Formal Organization: A Systems Approach* (Homewood, Ill.: The Dorsey Press, Inc., 1967).

Dubin, Robert, George C. Homans, Floyd C. Mann, and Delbert C. Miller. *Leadership and Productivity* (San Francisco: Chandler Publishing Company, 1965).

Gellerman, Saul W. *The Management of Human Relations* (New York: Holt, Rinehart and Winston, Inc., 1966).

Greenwood, William T. *Management and Organizational Behavior Theories* (Cincinnati: South-Western Publishing Company, 1965).

Hicks, Herbert G. *The Management of Organizations* (New York: McGraw-Hill Book Company, 1967).

Huneryager, S. G. and I. L. Heckmann. *Human Relations in Management,* rev. ed. (Cincinnati: South-Western Publishing Company, 1967).

Fleishman, Edwin A. *Studies in Personnel and Industrial Psychology,* rev. ed. (Homewood, Ill.: The Dorsey Press, Inc., 1967).

Likert, Rensis. *The Human Organization: Its Management and Value* (New York: McGraw-Hill Book Company, 1967).

Likert, Rensis. *New Patterns of Management* (New York: McGraw-Hill Book Company, 1961).

Litterer, Joseph A. *Organizations: Structure and Behavior* (New York: John Wiley & Sons, Inc., 1963).

Marrow, Alfred, et al. *Management by Participation* (New York: Harper & Row, Publishers, Incorporated, 1967).

Maslow, A. H. *Motivation and Personality* (New York: Harper & Row, Publishers, Incorporated, 1954).

McGregor, Douglas. *The Human Side of Enterprise* (New York: McGraw-Hill Book Company, 1960).

McGregor, Douglas. *The Professional Manager* (New York: McGraw-Hill Book Company, 1960).

Megginson, Leon C. *Personnel: A Behavioral Approach to Administration* (Homewood, Ill.: Richard D. Irwin, Inc., 1967).

Miner, John B. *Introduction to Industrial Clinical Psychology* (New York: McGraw-Hill Book Company, 1966).

Mullen, James H. *Personality and Productivity in Management* (New York: Columbia University Press, 1966).

Pigors, Paul, Charles A. Myers, and F. T. Malm (eds.). *Management of Human Resources* (New York: McGraw-Hill Book Company, 1968).

Sayles, Leonard R. and George Strauss. *Human Behavior in Organizations* (Englewood Cliffs, N.J.: Prentice-Hall, Inc., 1966).

Scott, William G. *Human Relations in Management* (Homewood, Ill.: Richard D. Irwin, Inc., 1962).

Seiler, John A. *Systems Analysis in Organizational Behavior* (Homewood, Ill.: The Dorsey Press, Inc., 1967).

Strauss, Geroge, and Leonard Sayles. *Personnel: The Human Problems of Management* (Englewood Cliffs, N.J.: Prentice-Hall, Inc., 1967).

Vroom, Victor H. *Motivation in Management* (American Foundation for Management Research, 1965).

APPENDIX A

NOTES ON PERSONNEL PROCESSES

A framework to use in the administration of personnel behavior, which has been described as a broad operational process, must be divided into a number of independent subprocesses. These processes must be constructed from terms generally accepted and clearly defined, as must be the subject matter being treated. The following subprocesses have been suggested as comprising the most vital aspects of personnel management.

THE PERSONNEL MANAGEMENT PROCESSES
by Wendell French[*]

THE LEADERSHIP PROCESS

The process of leadership is the personal influencing of individual and group behavior toward organizational objectives. It is a complex matter involving the traits, philosophy, and behavior of the leader, the characteristics and behavior of subordinates, the traits and behavior of the leader's superior, the goals of the organization, and the entire network of personnel subprocesses.

THE JUSTICE-DETERMINATION PROCESS

The process of justice determination is a flow of organizational events that allocates rewards and penalties to organizational members in proportion to their relative contribution and that corrects mistakes in such allocations. The administration of equity and justice is a matter that occupies a good deal of the time and energy of every manager. As in the age-old definition of justice, "equal treatment under the law," people working in organizations expect treatment based upon reasonable policies and rules applicable to the entire group of which they are part. Since most employees also have some concept of the importance of being treated as individuals as well as members of a group, what is just or fair becomes an exceedingly complex question, but a question with which all managers must deal.

In addition to being concerned with the *substance* of the decisions on human resources, people in organizations also tend to be concerned with the *procedures* used for determining what is equitable or fair. Further, they are

*Wendell French, *The Personnel Management Process: Human Resources Administration,* 2d. ed. (Boston: Houghton Mifflin Company, 1970), pp. 48-50. Reprinted by permission of the author and Houghton-Mifflin Co.

concerned with the kind and quality of the avenues of appeal open to them. Thus, both the quality of treatment and the procedures used in this treatment are important, and any discussion of organizational justice must include some emphasis on substantive and procedural matters pertaining to discipline, lay-offs, transfers, promotions, privileges, work schedules, and wages.

THE TASK-SPECIALIZATION PROCESS

Each organization encompasses a *flow of events into which the total task to be done is divided and through which the nature of individual jobs is determined.* This process is essentially synonymous with "designing the organization" or with the traditional management concept of "organizing." Of the various personnel processes we will be discussing, this one is probably the least specially identified with personnel management. Yet so much of personnel management is a direct reflection of this process that it is almost impossible to present a thorough treatment of the subject without some analysis of this flow of events.

In general, the task-specialization process consists of a sequence of events and activities as follows: (1) the determination of organizational objectives; (2) organizational planning, including design of the organization and job based on the tools, machines, and the systems technology to be used in achieving the enterprise's goals; (3) the communication of job design to members of the organization through the use of such devices as job descriptions and performance standards and through training and example; (4) the determination of human qualifications required on these jobs (job specifications); and (5) the establishment of work rules. Although each of these sub-aspects tends to stem from the preceding one, there is considerable reciprocal interdependence.

THE STAFFING PROCESS

The staffing process is a complex network of events that results in the continuous manning of the various jobs throughout the organization. In one sense, it is a flow of people into, and out of, the various jobs in the organization. The process typically includes the following activities: manpower planning, authorization for staffing, developing sources of applicants, applicant evaluation, employment decisions and offers, induction and orientation, assimilation, transfers, demotions, promotions, and separations. Some of the devices commonly used in the systems designed to facilitate this broad process are manning charts, application blanks, interviews, tests, reference checks, and performance appraisal devices.

THE APPRAISAL PROCESS

The process of appraisal is the continuous evaluation of individuals within the organization. Such evaluations are constantly being made for a variety of purposes, including selection, correction, training, pay increases, promotions, discipline, transfers, etc. Appraisals may vary from highly subjective, almost subconscious, evaluations to highly systematized reviews focusing on specific behavior.

THE COMPENSATION PROCESS

The process of compensation is a flow of events that determines the level of financial rewards and fringe benefits received by each member of the organization. This process includes the allocation of both financial and non-financial rewards. Typically found in this complex process is the use of some mechanism for assessing competitive wages in the external labor market, for job evaluation, for the establishment of wage rates and perhaps salary ranges in different job categories, and for some decision-making process in establishing salaries or wages according to differential performance. In addition, there will usually be extra payments for shift work, overtime, or "call in" work. There may also be some efforts directed to the stimulation of individual or group performance, or both, through incentive systems, profit-sharing, or bonuses. The provision of vacations, holidays, and other fringe benefits may also be considered important parts of the compensation process.

THE COLLECTIVE-BARGAINING PROCESS

The collective-bargaining process can be thought of as a complex network of events in the unionized organization, a network that serves to determine wages and fringe benefits, hours, and working conditions and that introduces a unique kind of transactional relationship between two institutions, the union and the employer. Not only does this flow of events have the purpose of reconciling the conflicting demands and requirements of both parties, but it is assumed to have broader social purposes, including minimizing labor strife and facilitating the flow of commerce.

Certain aspects of the collective bargaining process will be emphasized. Stressed, in particular, will be the process that culminates in the formation of a union, i.e., the unionization process; pre-negotiation strategies and tactics; negotiations between the union and management on wages, hours, and working conditions; the the process of administering the agreement, including grievance and arbitration proceedings.

THE ORGANIZATIONAL TRAINING AND DEVELOPMENT PROCESS

Organizational development is a new concept which is beginning to have a major impact on a significant number of organizations in the United States and abroad. Although some of its unique aspects will be discussed in subsequent chapters, the process will be defined here in *terms as a complex network of events that enhances the ability of an organization or of a subunit in an organization to be creative in solving problems and adapting to the external environment, and that enhances the organization's ability to foster a climate in which the capabilities of people can grow and develop.* In a broad sense, traditional programs in skill-training and managerial development are frequently part of this total process and will be considered as interrelated with it. Such matters as coaching and appraisal interviews can also be considered.

APPENDIX B

CURRENT LIBRARY MANPOWER
PHILOSOPHY AND B.B.P.S.

This appendix provides, through illustrations, a brief examination of selected current approaches to library manpower planning and procedures and permits a comparison of these concepts with BBPS. The first proposal represents a "task approach" to personnel administration. The normative approach to library education and manpower administration is illustrated with the statement by the Council of the American Library Association. The third concept explored in the appendix represents the "standard" approach.

THE TASK APPROACH

Reproduced below is a statement taken from the Appendix of the *School Library Personnel: Task Analysis Survey*. It is an example of a compilation resulting from job and task analysis. The larger report is a part of the School Library Manpower Project, a five-year program funded by the Knapp Foundation of North Carolina Incorporated and administered by the American Association of School Librarians. The program is designed to treat three aspects of the problem of developing and utilizing school library manpower: (1) task and job analysis, (2) education for school librarianship, and (3) recruitment.

TASKS PERFORMED *ONLY* BY PERSONNEL IN
PARTICULAR PAID STAFF POSITIONS[1]

Listed below are the tasks performed *only* by personnel in particular paid staff positions in one-half or more of the schools in the survey. For example, heads of library media centers performed the administrative task, "schedules use of facilities," in one-half or more of the participating elementary schools; no other staff person performed this task. These data, compiled by computer, further emphasize the tasks considered as major responsibilities of personnel in particular staff positions.

Only heads of library media centers and technicians were shown as performing tasks *not performed* by other personnel in one-half or more of the elementary schools in which they served. Heads of library media centers performed numerous tasks, particularly in the duty categories of development of educational program, administration, instruction, selection of materials and equipment, and special services to faculty and students; in contrast, technicians performed only two production tasks not performed by any other staff person in one-half or more of the elementary schools.

Heads of library media centers, audiovisual specialists, and clerks or aides were shown as performing tasks not performed by other personnel in one-half or more of the participating secondary schools in which they served. Personnel in these staff positions performed few tasks not performed by personnel in any other staff position. Both heads of centers and audiovisual specialists performed two tasks; clerks or aides performed the largest number—six.

Elementary-School Library Media Centers

HEADS OF LIBRARY MEDIA CENTERS

Development of educational program:
  Assists individual teachers in curriculum planning
  Plans cooperatively with faculty members to coordinate materials and
    library activities with curriculum programs, units, and textbooks
  Observes classroom work to coordinate library activities with school
    instructional programs
  Plans and discusses library-involved topics, units, and activities with teachers
  Works with teachers to design innovations in instruction

Administrative tasks:
  Plans arrangement of library space and furniture
  Schedules use of facilities
  Prepares library staff work schedules
  Assigns duties to library staff
  Supervises work of the professional library staff
  Develops necessary forms for operation of the library
  Submits reports to administration
  Determines rules for the conduct of students in the library
  Assumes responsibility for decisions concerning disciplinary actions
  Informs library staff of planned activities and requests
  Attends and participates in meetings of professional organizations

Instructional tasks:
  Orients students to the library
  Reviews library rules and procedures
  Plans sequential program of library instruction
  Gives incidental instruction in note-taking and outlining in connection
    with library work
  Gives incidental instruction in library skills
  Gives instruction in the use of materials
  Gives instruction in basic reference techniques
  Gives instruction in specialized reference books and other materials
    before class research project is begun
  Prepares exams in library skills
  Evaluates students' library skills and performance and informs teachers
    of results
  Assists with independent study
  Guides reference and research work of small and large groups

Selection of materials and equipment:

    Evaluates existing collections to determine needs

    Enlists faculty participation and recommendations in evaluating and selecting materials

    Reads books, magazines, professional journals, catalogs, and review sources for background information in selection of materials and equipment

    Evaluates and selects print materials

    Scans local publications and periodicals for resource materials and information

Acquisition of materials and equipment:

    Acknowledges gifts and exchanges

Organization of materials and equipment:

    Verifies preliminary filing of catalog and shelf list cards to complete filing

    Plans for reorganization and relocation of materials collections

Circulation of materials and equipment:

    Establishes policies and procedures for circulation of materials

Special services to faculty and students:

    Answers ready-reference questions

    Performs general reference services

    Initiates projects and activities relating to the library and its resources

    Introduces materials of special interest to class groups

    Suggests related materials, ideas, and resource people for classroom units

    Plans and conducts picture book hours

    Plans and conducts story hours

    Plans and directs special observances of book and library weeks, holidays, etc.

    Assists in and provides materials for extracurricular activities

    Develops with teachers a plan for pupils to follow in completing assignments

    Establishes with teachers procedures for mass assignments involving the use of the library

    Conducts class visits to the library

    Maintains schedules of class activities in library

    Orients faculty to the library program, materials, and services

    Informs teachers of new library services, materials, and equipment

    Promotes use of professional library

    Reads and reviews professional materials

    Introduces teachers to bibliographic tools in subject disciplines

    Assists teachers in locating bibliographic data

TECHNICIANS

Production of materials:

    Duplicates tape recordings

    Maintains, repairs, and makes minor adjustments to audiovisual equipment

Secondary-School Library Media Centers

HEADS OF LIBRARY MEDIA CENTERS
    Administrative tasks:
        Assigns duties to library staff
        Submits reports to administration

AUDIOVISUAL SPECIALISTS
    Administrative tasks:
        Trains student audiovisual aides
    Maintenance tasks:
        Maintains cumulative records of condition of and maintenance work
           on equipment

CLERKS OR AIDES
    Preparation of materials and equipment:
        Types cards, pockets, and labels for materials
    Maintenance of materials and equipment:
        Maintains bindery records
    Clerical and secretarial tasks:
        Handles clerical and secretarial aspects of correspondence
        Types notices, requisitions, bulletins, bibliographies, letters, stencils,
           orders, etc.
        Files orders and invoices
        Prepares adding machine tape to verify total costs of purchases

THE NORMATIVE APPROACH

The second concept is a general statement with which nearly everyone will agree. Librarians and library educators, sometimes quite properly, tend to accept such "motherhood" statements as the basis for library education programs and local manpower development. Since people, not tasks, activities, or technology, are the key to successful library programs, the statement tends to minimize the frustrations that result from people working with people. Granted it is a good basis for personnel policies, but it does not acknowledge the human behavior aspects which results in local library personnel problems.

LIBRARY EDUCATION AND MANPOWER[2]

A Statement of Policy Adopted by the Council of the American Library Association, June 30, 1970[3]

1 The purpose of the policy statement is to recommend categories of library manpower, and levels of training and education appropriate to the preparation of personnel for these categories, which will support the highest standards of library service for all kinds of libraries and the most effective use of the variety of manpower skills and qualifications needed to provide it.

2 Library service as here understood is concerned with knowledge and information in their several forms—their identification, selection, acquisition, preservation, organization, communication and interpretation, and with assistance in their use.

3 To meet the goals of library service, both professional and supportive staff are needed in libraries. Thus the library occupation is much broader than that segment of it which is the library profession, but the library profession has responsibility for defining the training and education required for the preparation of personnel who work in libraries at any level, supportive or professional.

4 Skills other than those of librarianship may also have an important contribution to make to the achievement of superior library service. There should be equal recognition in both the professional and supportive ranks for those individuals whose expertise contributes to the effective performance of the library.

5 A constant effort must be made to promote the most effective utilization of manpower at all levels, both professional and supportive. The tables on page 2 (Figure 1) suggest a set of categories which illustrate a means for achieving this end.

6 The titles recommended here represent categories or broad classifications, within which it is assumed that there will be several levels of promotional steps. Specific job titles may be used within any category: for example, catalogers, reference librarians, children's librarians would be included in either the "Librarian" or (depending upon the level of their responsibilities and qualifications) "Senior Librarian" categories; department heads, the director of the library, and certain specialists would presumably have the additional qualifications and responsibilities which place them in the "Senior Librarian" category.

7 Where specific job titles dictated by local usage and tradition do not make clear the level of the staff member's qualification and responsibility, it is recommended that reference to the ALA category title be used parenthetically to provide the clarification desirable for communication and reciprocity. For example:

REFERENCE ASSISTANT (Librarian)   HEAD CATALOGER (Senior Librarian)

LIBRARY AIDE (Library Technical Assistant)

Figure 1

CATEGORIES OF LIBRARY PERSONNEL—PROFESSIONAL

TITLE — For positions requiring:		BASIC REQUIREMENTS	NATURE OF RESPONSIBILITY
library-related qualifications	nonlibrary-related qualifications		
Senior Librarian	Senior Specialist	In addition to relevant experience, education beyond the M.A. [i.e., a master's degree in any of its variant designations: M.A., M.L.S., M.S.L.S., M.Ed., etc.] as: post-master's degree; Ph.D.; relevant continuing education in many forms	Top-level responsibilities, including but not limited to administration; superior knowledge of some aspect of librarianship, or of other subject fields of value to the library
Librarian	Specialist	Master's degree	Professional responsibilities including those of management, which require independent judgment, interpretation of rules and procedures, analysis of library problems, and formulation of original and creative solutions for them (normally utilizing knowledge of the subject field represented by the academic degree)

CATEGORIES OF LIBRARY PERSONNEL—SUPPORTIVE

TITLE		BASIC REQUIREMENTS	NATURE OF RESPONSIBILITY
Library Associate	Associate Specialist	Bachelor's degree (with or without course work in library science); OR bachelor's degree, plus additional academic work short of the master's degree (in librarianship for the Library Associate; in other relevant subject fields for the Associate Specialist)	Supportive responsibilities at a high level, normally working within the established procedures and techniques, and with some supervision by a professional, but requiring judgment, and subject knowledge such as is represented by a full, four-year college education culminating in the bachelor's degree
Library Technical Assistant	Technical Assistant	At least two years of college-level study; OR A.A. degree, with or without Library Technical Assistant training; OR postsecondary school training in relevant skills	Tasks performed as supportive staff to Associates and higher ranks, following established rules and procedures, and including, at the top level, supervision of such tasks
Clerk		Business school or commercial courses, supplemented by in-service training or on-the-job experience	Clerical assignments as required by the individual library

8 The title "Librarian" carries with it the connotation of "professional" in the sense that professional tasks are those which require a special background and education on the basis of which library needs are identified, problems are analyzed, goals are set, and original and creative solutions are formulated for them, integrating theory into practice, and planning, organizing, communicating, and administering successful programs of service to users of the library's materials and services. In defining services to users, the professional person recognizes potential users as well as current ones, and designs services which will reach all who could benefit from them.

9 The title "Librarian" therefore should be used only to designate positions in libraries which utilize the qualifications and impose the responsibilities suggested above. Positions which are primarily devoted to the routine application of established rules and techniques, however useful and essential to the effective operation of a library's ongoing services, should not carry the word "Librarian" in the job title.

10 It is recognized that every type and size of library may not need staff appointments in each of these categories. It is urged, however, that this basic scheme be introduced wherever possible to permit where needed the necessary flexibility in staffing.

11 The salaries for each category should offer a range of promotional steps sufficient to permit a career-in-rank. The top salary in any category should overlap the beginning salary in the next higher category, in order to give recognition to the value of experience and knowledge gained on the job.

12 Inadequately supported libraries or libraries too small to be able to afford professional staff should nevertheless have access to the services and supervision of a librarian. To obtain the professional guidance that they themselves cannot supply, such libraries should promote cooperative arrangements or join larger systems of cooperating libraries through which supervisory personnel can be supported. Smaller libraries which are part of such a system can often maintain the local service with building staff at the Associate level.

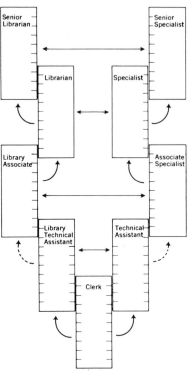

Figure 2

If one thinks of Career *Lattices* rather than Career *Ladders*, the flexibility intended by the Policy Statement may be better visualized. The movement among staff responsibilities, for example, is not necessarily directly up, but often may be lateral to increased responsibilities of equal importance. Each category embodies a number of promotional steps within it, as indicated by the gradation markings on each bar. The top of any category overlaps in responsibility and salary the next higher category.

Comments on the Categories

13 The *Clerk* classifications do not require formal academic training in library subjects. The assignments in these categories are based upon general clerical and secretarial proficiencies. Familiarity with basic library terminology and routines necessary to adapt clerical skills to the library's needs is best learned on the job.

14 The *Technical Assistant* categories assume certain kinds of specific "technical" skills; they are not meant simply to accommodate advanced clerks. While clerical skills might well be part of a Technical Assistant's equipment, the emphasis in his assignment should be on the special technical skill. For example, someone who is skilled in handling audiovisual equipment, or at introductory data processing, or in making posters and other displays might well be hired in the Technical Assistant category for these skills, related to librarianship only to the extent that they are employed in a library. A *Library*

Technical Assistant is a person with certain specifically library-related skills—in preliminary bibliographic searching for example, or utilization of certain mechanical equipment—the performance of whose duties seldom requires him to call upon a background in general education.

15 The *Associate* categories assume a need for an educational background like that represented by a bachelor's degree from a good four-year institution of higher education in the United States. Assignments may be such that library knowledge is less important than general education, and whether the title is *Library* Associate or Associate *Specialist* depends upon the nature of the tasks and responsibilities assigned. Persons holding the B.A. degree, with or without a library science minor or practical experience in libraries, are eligible for employment in this category. The title within the Associate category that is assigned to the individual will depend upon the relevance of his training and background to the specific assignment.

16 The Associate category also provides the opportunity for persons of promise and exceptional talent to begin library employment below the level of professional (as defined in this statement) and thus to combine employment in a library with course work at the graduate level. Where this kind of work/study arrangement is made, the combination of work and formal study should provide 1) increasing responsibility within the Associate ranks as the individual moves through the academic program, and 2) eligibility for promotion, upon completion of the master's degree, to positions of professional responsibility and attendant reclassification to the professional category.

17 The first professional category—*Librarian, or Specialist*—assumes responsibilities that are professional in the sense described in paragraph #8 above. A good liberal education plus graduate-level study in the field of specialization (either in librarianship or in a relevant field) are seen as the minimum preparation for the kinds of assignments implied. The title, however, is given for a position entailing professional responsibilities and not automatically upon achievement of the academic degree.

18 The *Senior* categories assume relevant professional experience as well as qualifications beyond those required for admission to the first professional ranks. Normally it is assumed that such advanced qualifications shall be held in some specialty, either in a particular aspect of librarianship or some relevant subject field. Subject specializations are as applicable in the *Senior Librarian* category as they are in the *Senior Specialist* category.

19 Administrative responsibilities entail advanced knowledge and skills comparable to those represented by any other high-level specialty, and appointment to positions in top administration should normally require the qualifications of a *Senior Librarian* with a specialization in administration. This category, however, is not limited to administrators, whose specialty is only one of several specializations of value to the library service. There are many areas of special knowledge within librarianship which are equally important and to which equal recognition in prestige and salary should be given. A highly qualified person with a specialist responsibility in some aspect of librarianship—archives, bibliography, reference, for example—should be eligible for advanced status and financial rewards without being forced to abandon for administrative responsibilities his area of major competence.

Implications for Formal Education

20 Until examinations are identified that are valid and reliable tests of equivalent qualifications, the academic degree (or evidence of years of academic work completed) is recommended as the single best means for determining that an applicant has the background recommended for each category.

21 In the selection of applicants for positions at any level, and for admission to library schools, attention should be paid to personal aptitudes and qualifications in addition to academic ones. The nature of the position or specialty, and particularly the degree to which it entails working with others, with the public, or with special audiences or materials should be taken into account in the evaluation of a prospective student or employee.

22 As library services change and expand, as new audiences are reached, as new media take on greater importance in the communication process, and as new approaches to the handling of materials are introduced, the kinds of preparation required of those who will be employed in libraries will become more varied. Degrees in fields other than librarianship will be needed in the Specialist categories. For many Senior Librarian positions, an advanced degree in another subject field rather than an additional degree in librarianship, may be desirable. Previous experience need not always have been in libraries to have pertinence for appointment in a library.

23 Because the principles of librarianship are applied to the materials of information and knowledge broader than any single field, and because they are related to subject matter outside of librarianship itself, responsible education in these principles should be built upon a broad rather than a narrowly specialized background education. To the extent that courses in library science are introduced in the four-year, undergraduate program, they should be concentrated in the last two years and should not constitute a major inroad into course work in the basic disciplines: the humanities, the sciences, and the social sciences.

24 Training courses for Library Technical Assistants at the junior or community college level should be recognized as essentially terminal in intent (or as service courses rather than a formal program of education), designed for the preparation of supportive rather than professional staff. Students interested in librarianship as a career should be counselled to take the general four-year college course rather than the specific two-year program, with its inevitable loss of time and transferable content. Graduates of the two-year programs are not prohibited from taking the additional work leading to the bachelor's and master's degrees, provided they demonstrate the necessary qualifications for admission to the senior college program, but it is an indirect and less desirable way to prepare for a professional career, and the student should be so informed.

25 Emphasis in the two-year Technical Assistant programs should be more on skills training than on general library concepts and procedures. In many cases it would be better from the standpoint of the student to pursue more broadly-based vocational courses which will teach technical skills applicable in a variety of job situations rather than those limited solely to the library setting.

26 Undergraduate instruction in library science other than training courses for Library Technical Assistants should be primarily a contribution to liberal education rather than an opportunity to provide technological and methodological training. This does not preclude the inclusion of course work related to the basic skills of library practice, but it does affect teaching method and approach, and implies an emphasis on the principles that underlie practice rather than how-to-do-it, vocational training.

27 Certain practical skills and procedures at all levels are best learned on the job rather than in the academic classroom. These relate typically to details of operation which may vary from institution to institution, or to routines which require repetition and practice for their mastery. The responsibility for such in-service parts of the total preparation of both librarians and supportive staff rests with libraries and library systems rather than with the library schools.

28 The objective of the master's programs in librarianship should be to prepare librarians capable of anticipating and engineering the change and improvement required to move the profession constantly forward. The curriculum and teaching methods should be designed to serve this kind of education for the future rather than to train for the practice of the present.

29 Certain interdisciplinary concepts (information science is an example) are so intimately related to the basic concepts underlying library service that they properly become a part of the library school curriculum rather than simply an outside specialty. Where such content is introduced into the library school it should be incorporated into the entire curriculum, enriching every course where it is pertinent. The stop-gap addition of individual courses in such a specialty, not integrated into the program as a whole, is an inadequate assimilation of the intellectual contribution of the new concept to library education and thinking.

30 In recognition of the many areas of related subject matter of importance to library service, library schools should make knowledge in other fields readily available to students, either through the appointment of staff members from other disciplines or through permitting students to cross departmental, divisional, and institutional lines in reasoned programs in related fields. Intensive specializations at the graduate level, building upon strengths in the parent institution or the community, are a logical development in professional library education.

31 Library schools should be encouraged to experiment with new teaching methods, new learning devices, different patterns of scheduling and sequence, and other means, both traditional and nontraditional, that may increase the effectiveness of the students' educational experience.

32 Research has an important role to play in the educational process as a source of new knowledge both for the field of librarianship in general and for library education in particular. In its planning, budgeting, and organizational design, the library school should recognize research, both theoretical and applied, as an imperative responsibility.

Continuing Education

33 Continuing Education is essential for all library personnel, professional and supportive, whether they remain within a position category or are preparing to move into a higher one. Continuing education opportunities include both formal and informal learning situations, and need not be limited to library subjects or the offerings of library schools.

34 The "continuing education" which leads to eligibility for Senior Librarian or Specialist positions may take any of the forms suggested directly above so long as the additional education and experience are relevant to the responsibilities of the assignment.

35 Library administrators must accept responsibility for providing support and opportunities (in the form of leaves, sabbaticals, and released time) for the continuing education of their staffs.

THE COLOR BOOK APPROACH

A third approach to library personnel administration will be referred to as the "color book approach." This approach is used in two American Library Association publications, *Personnel Organization and Procedure; A Manual Suggested for Use in College and University Libraries* and *Personnel Organization and Procedure; A Manual Suggested for Use in Public Libraries.* The manuals are "theoretical" statements written by a committee of "professionals."

The purpose of this manual is twofold: First to treat systematically all of the generally accepted basic principles and procedures of sound personnel administration which should be considered by heads of libraries so that they can be clearly stated to, and fully understood by, members of the library staff. Second, to provide in this publication an example of such a statement written within a specific, if imaginary, framework as an actual personnel manual or handbook. We hope by this approach to make it easier for library administrators to prepare similar statements, incorporating such changes as are appropriate to differences in local situations.[4]

Recognizing that the attainment of interpersonal conflict is a complex phenomenon, one can readily see the superficiality of a statement which attributes need satisfaction to an external set of personnel policies and procedures. Below are examples of the kinds of conclusions one sometimes hears as a result of an individual as well as a comparative analysis of the two manuals.

1. Each manual could become a local personnel organization and procedure manual through a retyping of the document and the completion of appropriate blanks. Blanks are provided on pages seven, eight, nine, ten, fifteen, eighteen, and twenty of *Public Libraries*[5] and seven, eight, nine, ten, fourteen, seventeen, eighteen, and nineteen of *Academic Libraries.*[6]

2. The majority of the material in both volumes, although done by different committees, is the same. This is particularly true for such important topics as appointments, development of staff, performance evaluation, promotions, transfers, demotions, tenure, separation from service, and working conditions. In fact, certain sections are exactly the same. Compare, for example, pages fifteen and sixteen of *Public Libraries* with fourteen and fifteen of *Academic Libraries* on the important topics of performance evaluations, promotions, transfers, demotions, and tenure. The first five paragraphs are identical.

3. The way personnel policies are perceived by the employees, the way they are administered, the pressures of the chief librarian, the informal group, and the union, and the individual needs of employees are not the major factors contributing to effective employee performance.

4. If the chief librarian knows how to develop a personnel policy and procedure manual, he knows all there is to know about personnel administration.

5. Personal needs of library employees vary little from library to library; therefore, standard procedures and policies can be adopted.

6. The right answer in one personnel situation is the right answer in another; therefore, the personnel administrator becomes equipped to solve personnel problems through universally applicable solutions.

If a library administrator has taken steps to duplicate one of the above manuals in hopes that its adoption would improve employees' perform-ance but found that it did not, a possible reason for failure is that justice, decency, managerial behavior, and effective conflict resolution cannot be written in such personnel manuals. They must be written in the mind and the heart of the library administrator or supervisor. The Eberhard Library had such a manual, but it was derived from a topsy-turvy view of organizational behavior. Completing blanks and copying all the right statements lacks the insight the administrator must gain from the frustrations, negotiations, trades, bargaining, and assessment of the state of an organization. The "color book" approach is too easy. It allows librarians promoted to administrative positions to qualify for such promotions by purely academic, professional, or technical qualification. Such statements rely too heavily upon a "how to do it" approach and minimize the cause-and-effect relationship between need satisfaction and job performance.

FOOTNOTES

[1] Research Division, National Education Association, *School Library Personnel: Task Analysis Survey* (Chicago: American Library Association, 1969). A report prepared in Phase I of the School Library Manpower Project by the Research Division of the National Education Association in a national study to identify the tasks performed by school library personnel in unified service programs at the building level. (Copyright, 1969, by the American Library Association, all rights reserved.) pp. 87-89.

[2] Reprinted by Permission of the American Library Association.

[3] Throughout this statement, wherever the term "librarianship" is used, it is meant to be read in its broadest sense as encompassing the relevant concepts of information science and documentation; wherever the term "libraries" is used, the current models of media centers, learning centers, educational resources centers, information, documentation, and referral centers are also assumed. To avoid the necessity of repeating the entire gamut of variations and expansions, the traditional library terminology is employed in its most inclusive meaning.

[4] American Library Association, *Personnel Organization and Procedure: A Manual Suggested for Use in Public Libraries,* 2d. ed. (Chicago: ALA, 1968), Preface, or American Library Association, *Personnel Organization and Procedure: A Manual Suggested for Use in Academic Libraries,* 2d. ed. (Chicago: ALA, 1968), Preface.

[5] *Ibid.*

[6] *Ibid.*